Old High German Literature

Twayne's World Authors Series

Ulrich Weisstein, Editor of German Literature
Indiana University

TWAS 688

Codex 136, fol. 85ʳ of the Cathedral Library at Merseburg (reproduced by kind permission of the Stiftsarchivar of the Domstift Merseburg). On an originally blank page of a ninth-century liturgical book, one scribe of the tenth century has written the two Merseburg Charms in Old High German, and another had added a liturgical blessing in Latin. The charms are pagan in content and the blessing is, of course, Christian.

Old High German Literature

By Brian O. Murdoch

Stirling University

Twayne Publishers • *Boston*

Old High German Literature

Brian O. Murdoch

Copyright © 1983 by G.K. Hall & Company
All Rights Reserved
Published by Twayne Publishers
A Division of G. K. Hall & Company
70 Lincoln Street
Boston, Massachusetts 02111

Book Production by Marne B. Sultz

Book Design by Barbara Anderson

Printed on permanent/durable acid-free
paper and bound in the United States of
America.

Library of Congress Cataloging in Publication Data

Murdoch, Brian, 1944–
    Old High German literature.

    (Twayne's world authors series ; TWAS 688)
    Bibliography: pp. 146–154
    Includes index.
    1. German literature–Old High German, 750-1050–
History and criticism I. Title. II. Series.
PT183.M85   1983 .   830'.9'001   82-25478
ISBN 0-8057-6535-2

To my parents

Contents

About the Author

Brian Murdoch was born in London in 1944. He studied German and Russian at Exeter University, and then took his doctorate at Cambridge, writing on early medieval German poetry. He has taught German at Glasgow University, the University of Illinois at Chicago Circle, and he is at present senior lecturer and head of the German department at the University of Stirling (Scotland). He is married and has two children.

He has published a number of books and articles on medieval German (and also Celtic) literature, concentrating in particular on religious writings, most notably the legends of Adam and Eve. In 1976 he coauthored a volume in the German *Sammlung Metzler* on Old High German poetry. He has also published books and articles concerned with modern German and European literature, and he has a number of regular reviewing and editorial commitments.

Preface

The term "Old High German" belongs primarily to the study of language, not of literature. It is applied to the earliest stage of the German language, as found in written documents from the middle of the eighth century to the middle of the eleventh, when a series of major changes give rise to the quite distinct second stage of German, which we call Middle High German. Even "Old High German" does not refer to a unified language, but rather to a group of dialects, sometimes markedly different from one another, but sharing certain linguistic features not found in other languages.

To speak of a literature in Old High German is also problematic. A certain number of vernacular German texts, written down between about 750 and about 1050, have survived, but can they be referred to as literature? Certainly some poetry is included, but the prose is virtually all unoriginal, translated from Latin; furthermore, much of it is not even connected prose at all, but collections of single-word glosses.

In the period in question, writing in German at all was a novelty. The predominant—indeed, the only—literary language in Germany in the period is Latin. Compared with a very large amount of Latin writing, the German survivals are very few indeed. Latin was the language in which literature was written for official preservation, and the use of the word "survival" for the German texts is apt. The German writings either arise from and depend completely upon Latin originals, as parallel translations, or as words simply written between the lines of the Latin; or if they are original, then they have usually survived because someone used a blank page in a Latin manuscript, or even a wide margin, to jot down, sometimes rather carelessly, a few lines in German. When in the ninth century the first named German poet, Otfrid of Weissenburg, composed a long poem on the life of Christ, he felt the need to apologize (in Latin) to his ecclesiastical superior for having done so in a language that he refers to as "rough and uncultivated."

But Otfrid *did* write a German work, a work of enormous importance as the first full-length conscious literary product in that language. Three full manuscripts of it survive (one with corrections by the author himself), and there were others. They were carefully and indeed beautifully written, and they were circulated beyond Otfrid's own monastery. Otfrid's work is the central point of this book, the first milestone in the emergence of German as a literary language. To chart that emergence, it is necessary to examine the functional writings of the early days of Christianity in Germany, to observe how German words are employed (and created) to convey new and complex ideas, to see then how a smooth and comprehensible prose style becomes possible, and to note the development of vocabulary and of a self-conscious written literature.

Otfrid's work is Christian, and the emergence of written literature is bound up completely with the work of the church in early medieval Germany. There must have been a pre-Christian poetic tradition in German, but this must have been oral. We are told of such oral poetry in Latin writings, and we may guess from the study of Old Norse or Old English that a number of oral poems existed, but only one has survived in German, in a Christianized form, and presumably written down by monks. In the late nineteenth century, the literary scholar Rudolf Koegel constructed an entire volume of a large-scale literary history around this one text, referring in detail to other works which he presumed to have existed once. Such an approach is no longer acceptable. Old High German literature can only mean the German literature composed or recorded by representatives of the church in early medieval Germany. We owe to the efforts of members of the Latin church even the small glimpse of the heroic world afforded us by the *Lay of Hildebrand.*

For the Middle Ages, a purely aesthetic concept of literature is inappropriate. The great majority of the Old High German survivals are functional. The glosses and translations, of course, elucidate the Latin originals, even if they also contribute to the development of German as a vehicle for written communication. Apart from the *Lay of Hildebrand,* too, the poetic writings were nearly all composed *ad maiorem Dei gloriam,* to teach as well as to please. Perhaps the clearest overlap between art and functionality is seen in the charms and blessings (which can be pagan or Christian). These often take the form of poetic texts which are nonetheless designed to heal, in part at least, by means of the magic of their words and word-patterns.

If the German material as such is small compared to the contemporary Latin writings, it is still very diverse, and some simplification is necessary if a complete picture is to be presented. Thus it is more valuable to describe one representative example of an interlinear gloss, to show what it *is,* rather than to enumerate all the known examples. In a monograph which deals with a single author, too, the general background need be given only once. Here, a background of facts has to be given almost for each individual work, since they were written in different literary centers—monasteries—isolated from one another.

One last point to be borne in mind is that Old High German literature is a manuscript literature. Otfrid's Gospel-poem was carefully written, but he conceived the work as a manuscript—print was still many centuries in the future. Otfrid wanted to make his point as an author not with the words alone, but with the layout, with different types of capital letters, with marginalia. A modern printed edition cannot imitate this. With other works the problem is more acute. In the case of the glosses or the translations, editors frequently, indeed usually, print just the German parts, allowing us to forget the presence of the Latin, which was there next to the German in the manuscript. The poems, too, have had to be edited. This is, of course, necessary, but decisions made by an individual editor (even on something as apparently trivial as capitalization, or line-division) need not necessarily be the only answers possible. Modern printed texts (and certainly modern translations) are often quite different from the manuscript version; and we can hardly ever tell how close that manuscript version was to the presumed original. The study of Old High German poses more problems than it solves, especially in this area.

The emphasis of this book is on the cultural and literary implications of the emergent literary language. In one sense the writing of a history of Old High German literature is a rash undertaking, since there is no continuous linear development. Both Otfrid in the ninth century and Notker of St. Gallen in the eleventh thought of themselves as innovators by using German in their writings, and both of them apologized for it. We may, however, outline the different traditions, and we may draw attention to the fresh starts, while maintaining a rough chronological sequence. A focus is provided by the Latin church, for which most of the works were composed, and by whose members most of them were written down.

I owe thanks to my colleagues at Stirling university, Dr. L. G. Jillings, Dr. B. Thompson, and Dr. M. Read, for their help and encouragement. For medical information used in Chapter 4 I am indebted to my friend C. Cameron of Glasgow and to Dr. C. Newman of the London Royal College of Physicians. The chapter in question, on the charms, was presented at the Denys Hay Seminar on Medieval and Renaissance History, at the University of Edinburgh early in 1981, and I profited from the discussion by those scholars present. Of the many specialists who have been kind enough to keep me in touch with their work, I might name D. R. McLintock, Professor Werner Schröder, Professor Ute Schwab, and Miss Hilda Swinburne. Errors, of course, remain my own. I owe, finally, a debt of gratitude to my wife, Ursula, for her continued support and assistance.

Stirling University   Brian O. Murdoch

Chronology

A chronology of Old High German literature can only be very tentative. We may estimate with some claim to accuracy the date of the manuscript transmission of individual works, but guessing at the date of *composition* is very much more difficult. Some texts, such as the charms, are simply undatable. Charms are found throughout the Old High German language period and beyond, and the Merseburg Charms, for example, written down in the tenth century, are pre-Christian in content and potentially very much older. This chronology attempts a rough dating for the major works, and adds those historical dates likely to be the most relevant to the study of the Old High German writings.

A.D.

410	Rome falls to the Visigoths.
453	Death of Attila the Hun.
454	Birth of Theoderic the Ostrogoth.
476	Odoacer ruler of Rome.
493	Theoderic kills Odoacer and assumes sovereignty in Rome; dies in 526.
561–584	Chilperic King of the Franks.
6th century	Earliest compilation of *Lex Salica.*
6th–7th century	*Southern Germanic runic inscriptions.*
7th century	Irish mission to Southern Germany.
643	*Edict of Rothar* (Lombardic).
8th century	Anglo-Saxon Mission to Germany.
732	Charles Martel defeats forces of Islam at Poitiers.
771	Charlemagne becomes King of the Franks; annexes Lombardy, 774; absorbs Bavaria, 778; crowned emperor in Rome, 800; conquers Frisians and Saxons, 804; dies, 814.

789	Admonitio Generalis.
794	Synod of Frankfurt.
814–840	Lewis I (the Pious), emperor.
from 8th century	*Old High German versions of prayers, catechisms, vows. Partial and full glosses. Charms* (some date from earlier period, perhaps). *Legal compilations with German terms.*
later 8th century	*Abrogans, Vocabularius Sancti Galli.*
late 8th/ early 9th century	*Isidore-translation, Mon(d)see Fragments.*
early 9th century	*Samanunga. Benedictine Rule glossed in full. Murbach Hymn glosses. Wessobrunn Prayer. Basle medical recipes.*
822–842	Hrabanus Maurus abbot of Fulda; dies as archbishop of Mainz, 856.
ca. 825–850	*Tatian-translation. Heliand* (Old Saxon). *Hildebrandslied-manuscript.*
839–871	Salomo bishop of Constance.
842	*Strasbourg Oaths.*
843	Partition of Verdun; Lothar I confirmed as emperor (840–855); Charles II (the Bald) king of France (West Franks), dies 877; Lewis II (the German) king of Germany (East Franks), dies 876.
ca. 860–870	*Otfrid's Gospel-Book.*
863–889	Liutbert archbishop of Mainz.
later 9th century	*Cologne Inscription, Sigihart's Prayers.*
876–882	Lewis III king of Germany.
877–879	Lewis II king of France.
879–882	Lewis III king of France, jointly with his brother Carloman (died 884).
881/2	*Ludwigslied.*
884–887	Charles III (the Fat) emperor of reunited territory.
late 9th/ early 10th century	*Georgslied. Petruslied.*

10th century	*Psalm 138 in German. Paris Phrasebook. Christ and the Samaritan Woman. Manuscript of the Merseburg Charms.*
ca. 950–1022	Notker Labeo (the German) of St. Gallen.
936–973	Otto I (the Great) emperor of Germany.
941	Henry, Otto's brother, reconciled with him and created Duke of Bavaria in 947; dies 955.
973–983	Otto II emperor of Germany.
983–1002	Otto III emperor of Germany.
985	Henry the Quarrelsome, reconciled with Otto III, re-created Duke Henry II of Bavaria; dies 995.
1002	Duke Henry IV of Bavaria, son of Henry the Quarrelsome, elected emperor of Germany as Henry II; dies 1024.
early 11th century	*De Heinrico* (?). *Summarium Heinrici.*
1048	Williram abbot of Ebersberg; dies 1085.
1070	Death of Otloh of St. Emmeram.
later 11th century	*Ezzos Gesang, Memento Mori, Vienna Genesis, prose Physiologus, Merigarto.*
1075	Death of Anno, archbishop of Cologne; proclaimed a saint 1183.
1095	Death of Noker of Zwiefalten.
early 12th century	*Annolied.*
12th century	*Konrad's Roland. Lamprecht's Alexander.*

Abbreviations

Most of the shorter Old High German works are found in one or more of the anthologies for which abbreviations are given below, and to which references are noted in the body of the text. Line-numbers and citations are from Steinmeyer's collection unless otherwise indicated. An abbreviation is also used for the major collection of glosses, but details of other editions are found in the notes. Bible references are to the Latin Vulgate, with English citation from the Douai version. Personal names are given in their English forms. Abbreviations for some frequently cited periodicals are used to avoid overburdening the notes.

Anthologies

MSD	Müllenhoff, Karl, and Scherer, Wilhelm. *Denkmäler deutscher Poesie und Prosa aus dem VIII–XII Jahrhundert.* 3d ed. by E. v. Steinmeyer. Berlin: Weidmann, 1892. 2 volumes. Reprinted as 4th ed. Berlin and Zurich: Weidmann, 1964.
St.	Steinmeyer, Elias v. *Die kleineren althochdeutschen Sprachdenkmäler.* Berlin: Weidmann, 1916. Reprinted as 2d ed. Berlin and Zurich: Weidmann, 1963.
Lb.	Braune, Wilhelm. *Althochdeutsches Lesebuch.* 16th ed. by E. A. Ebbinghaus. Tübingen: Niemeyer, 1978.

Glosses

Ahd. Gl.	Steinmeyer, Elias v. and Sievers, Eduard. *Die althochdeutschen Glossen.* Berlin: Weidmann, 1879–1922. 5 volumes.

Periodicals

PBB	*Beiträge zur Geschichte der deutschen Sprache und Literatur.*
RVjb	*Rheinische Vierteljahrsblätter.*
ZfdA	*Zeitschrift für deutsches Altertum.*
ZfdPh	*Zeitschrift für deutsche Philologie.*

Chapter One
Old High German Literature?

Toward the end of the ninth century, a Benedictine monk named Otfrid, from the monastery of Weissenburg, completed a poem on the life of Christ, in over seven thousand lines of German verse. His poem has survived in three complete and finely produced manuscripts, one of them corrected by Otfrid himself. For all that, the author still felt it necessary to justify, in a Latin letter to his church superior, and in German in the poem itself, the very act of writing such a work in his mother tongue. He was conscious of the literary and linguistic novelty of his work, and aware of a number of problems. He did not, however, really think of himself as writing in German. In the poem, he speaks of the language as "Frankish," using a tribal designation, not a national one, and the place at which this first intentionally preserved major literary work in German was written is now called Wissembourg, in French Alsace.

Recent studies of the earliest German literature have drawn attention to a lack of continuity in development, and to the fact that more than one writer regarded himself as an innovator.[1] Writers in German were indeed isolated, and even taking account of the fact that some material may have been lost, writings in Old High German are relatively few in number—indeed, very few compared with contemporaneous Latin works. All the poetry, including Otfrid's work, could be accommodated in a single volume. The prose might take up a little more room but, if shorn of the scholarly apparatus that nowadays accompanies it, would hardly fill a library shelf.

The written material that has survived in Old High German, then, is not on the face of it conducive to the production of a literary history. This seems even more problematic when we face the difficulty of establishing what the Old High German language itself actually *is*. There are fairly sound philological reasons, well-documented sound changes that place the cut-off point, the time at which Old High German gave way to another stage of the German language, in the middle of the eleventh century.

1

Where it begins, however, is unclear, since those beginnings seem to lie before the introduction of writing for the German language. Even the term "Old High German" is one of convenience. The standard grammar of the written language declares itself to be based upon a compromise: "There is . . . no such thing as a unified Old High German, no 'normal' language; it is purely a matter of practicality when learning the language that we begin with the East Franconian dialect . . . and that we use its forms for grammatical or lexical examples. There is no supra-dialectal standard written language."[2]

And yet "Old High German" was originally a philological term. It was used in the nineteenth century to describe the language of the earliest German texts. Every element in the term requires justification. That it is "High German" depends upon a series of sound changes, some of which took place before any of the documents in question were written down, and which separate this, the earliest stage of German, from the ancestors of modern English and Dutch. The changes are usually referred to collectively as the "High German sound shift." The reasons for its occurrence, and the date and place of origin, remain unclear. At this early period, even "German" presents a problem. While most of the writings with which we are here concerned were written in the geographical area which now comprises Germany, Austria, and Switzerland, this is not true of all of them. Modern geographical concepts fail to serve even as a rough guide.

The Peoples

What is meant by "Old High German," then, is the group of dialects spoken by a variety of Germanic tribes, all of these dialects having been affected to some degree at least by the High German sound shift, an irregular set of changes affecting certain sounds, which was well under way by the middle of the eighth century, and had probably begun in the early sixth. The Germanic tribes, including those whose languages underwent these changes, engaged in migrations and shifts of political power that continued well into the period of written literature.

The Germanic tribes to the North and East of the Roman empire fell into several more or less distinct linguistic groups, separated from each other at a very early stage. The languages of the group called "North Germanic" included the ancestors of the modern Scandinavian languages. "East Germanic" is applied to the languages spoken by a number of tribes who moved first of all southeastward into Europe from the Baltic. All of these tongues are extinct, and only one, Gothic, is at all well documented.

The Goths settled in the area around the Black Sea, and later a part of the tribe moved westward from there. Rome was attacked by these Western Goths, the Visigoths, in 410; and they settled ultimately in Spain, their powerful political unit falling only in 711 to the forces of Islam. Other East Germanic tribes included the Gepids, annihilated in the sixth century; the Vandals, whose African kingdom, conquered by the Byzantine emperor Justinian in 533, shows the extent of geographical movement involved; and the Burgundians, who settled eventually in the area around Worms, in present-day West Germany, moving south toward the Mediterranean rather later. Only isolated words or names remain in most of their languages.

The remaining Germanic tribes used to be classified conveniently as the "West Germanic" group, but the tribes involved—those most important to our study—are now seen as three related but separate subgroups: first, the "North-Sea Germans," which includes the Angles, Saxons, and Frisians; second, the "Weser-Rhine Germans," the Franks, Hessians, and Thuringians; and finally the "Elbe Germans," Bavarians, Alamans, and Lombards (Langobards). The second and third groups contain all the tribes whose dialects were affected by the High (a geographical term, referring to a more mountainous homeland) German sound shift.

The end of the fifth century is a convenient starting-point for a brief historical survey of these tribes. The final disintegration of the Roman empire in the West had taken place, and the most important of these tribes, the Franks, were at the beginning of a period of expansion which would lead, albeit erratically, to the so-called *translatio imperii ad Francos* ("the empire transferred to the Franks"), Charlemagne's supposed reconstitution of a new and holy Roman empire at the start of the ninth century.

The northernmost part of Germany, together with southern Denmark, was occupied at this time by the Frisians, the Angles, and the Saxons, and members of the last two groups were already beginning to move to England. The Saxons occupied the most easterly position, but covered large areas in the north of both parts of modern Germany. Below them were the Thuringians, whose territories extended as far as the Main, and below them, on the southeast borders between Germanic and Slav territories, was a relatively new confederation of smaller tribes, the Bavarians. Further south, in what is now Austria, were the Lombards, who moved into Italy in the sixth century, where they came into conflict with the Goths. Although the role of the Lombards in the history of Old High German literature is small, their contact with the Goths is an important channel of cultural transmission. Politically they were successful in Italy.

A Lombard kingdom there (which soon adopted the local, Romance, language) lasted until the eighth century, and the Lombardic duchies of Spoleto and Benevento, in southern Italy, lasted even longer. The final tribe—again more accurately a confederation of tribes—was the Alemannic group, whose name means literally "all men." These were a long-established group, and in the late fifth century their lands extended from Alsace to Switzerland, covering what is now Swabia (although the division of early Alemannic into linguistic subgroups including Swabian uses later names for only partially documented dialects). At this time the Alemannic confederation was growing and, having pushed upward toward Trier, was coming into conflict with the Franks.[3]

To that northern confederation, the Franks, was to fall the political hegemony over most of the tribes. These seem to have originated in an area between Utrecht and Mainz, and fell into two main groups, the Ripuarian Franks, in the area around Cologne, and the Salian Franks, later the dominant partners, who settled around Arras and Tournai. In the fifth century they had extended their lands well into Roman Gaul, and the expansion continued under the most powerful of the early Salian kings, Clovis (482–511), who, as king of Tournai, overthrew what was left of the Roman administration in northern France and established himself in an area which became known as Neustria, or West Francia, centering upon Paris. Clovis also embraced Christianity, specifically Catholic Christianity, as opposed to the Arian faith espoused by the Goths and the Burgundians.

Clovis was the first notable king of the house known (after an earlier member) as the Merovingians, but he was neither a king nor an emperor in any modern sense, simply a powerful local chieftain. The Franks suffered, moreover, from the Salian tradition of dividing inherited property equally among surviving sons, which almost always led to internecine fighting. Nevertheless, the Franks were able to assert their power in the next few centuries over the neighboring tribes. Clovis repulsed the Alemannic attack, and he also took Aquitaine from the Arian Visigoths in the name of Catholic Christianity. He attacked, but did not take, Burgundy.

The expansion continued in the sixth century. The Thuringians were defeated in 531, the Burgundians in 534, and the Bavarians in 555. By the mid-seventh century, the Frankish kingdoms covered most of present-day France, the Low Countries, Germany, Switzerland, and Austria. The plural—kingdoms—is important, however, and there was continued conflict among the Frankish rulers of Neustria, of Austrasia (the eastern side of the Rhine, what is now central Germany), of Aquitaine, and of

Burgundy. Unity, and the control of the more or less hostile subordinated tribes, called for firm rule, and this arose eventually in Austrasia, the "German" side of the Rhine, where the Germanic Frankish language was maintained. In the west the Germanic language gradually gave way to the Gallo-Roman ancestor of modern French.

The ruling dynasty that reunited the fragmented Frankish kingdoms was that of the Carolingians, named for Charles Martel, "the Hammer," who was technically a steward, a mayor of the palace for a by now only nominal Merovingian king. Charles is celebrated in particular for his victory, at Poitiers in 732, over Islam, a battle of great significance for European history as a whole, and one undertaken initially in defense of Aquitaine, over which he then assumed control. His son, Pippin, assumed full regal style and power as king of the Franks, and insofar as he was assisted in this by the Pope (for whom he established a papal state in Italy under Frankish protection), the seeds of the new Holy Roman Empire were already sown.

Pippin was succeeded by two sons, one of whom, later known as Charlemagne, Charles the Great, became sole ruler in 771. By then Aquitaine, Burgundy, Thuringia, and the Alemannic territories had been brought under control. Charlemagne annexed Lombardy in 774 (with the duchy of Spoleto, although Benevento remained independent) and absorbed the duchy of Bavaria in 778. He conquered some of northern Spain (by then in Arab hands), and both Brittany and Sardinia joined voluntarily a Frankish empire which even included Corsica and the Baleares. In the north, Charlemagne conquered the Frisians and Saxons by 804, and established his sovereignty over an area of very considerable size. It is under his influence, too, that we find the real beginnings of German writing, linked completely with the (sometimes enforced) spread and consolidation of the Christianity embraced by Clovis in 496. In 800 the Pope crowned Charlemagne emperor, in Rome, of an area some of which had never known Roman rule.[4]

As far as German is concerned, a written vernacular now arose for the first time, strictly in the service of the Christian mission and the Frankish state. The beginning was small, and not literary in a modern sense, but it was necessary for the development of literary and philosophical writing in German later on, a development on a larger scale than that of the oral material (a very little of which is preserved in later form) which may be assumed to have gone before.

Politically, however, Charlemagne's achievement did not last. After his death in 814 "the momentum he had imparted to his creation disguised for a while its lack of governmental machinery."[5] But not long after the great empire was divided into approximations of modern France and Germany, and the political power of the Franks even in the German-speaking areas was of limited duration.

High German

The High German sound shift affected the language of all the Elbe Germans and most of the Weser-Rhine Germans, but none of the North-Sea Germans. The ancestor of modern English was not affected, and English may still be used to demonstrate unshifted sounds. The changes, then, are found in the written documents of the Lombards, Bavarians, and Alamans in the south, and in those of most of the Franks. The Thuringians may be left out of consideration at this point, as we have no written evidence of their dialect (beyond a few names) until a later period.

The major sound changes concerned affected the stops in early Germanic, the sounds *p, t,* and *k,* with their voiced equivalents, *b, d, g.* Depending upon their position in a given word, the unvoiced stops shifted as follows: the sound *p* shifted to *pf* or *f(f)*—spellings vary when the sound comes to be written down; *t* shifted to the sound still written as *z* (ts) in modern German, and frequently like that in Old High German, or to the forerunner of modern German *s, ss,* or *ß*, again written in the early stages as *z(z)* very frequently; the *k* sound shifted to a Germanic *h,* written that way, with some variation, in the earliest writings, and representing a modern German *ch.* Sometimes it was shifted to a very guttural *kh,* and once more, spellings vary. Of the voiced stops, a single *b* remained unshifted for the most part, although it became *p* in some southern dialects, as it did when doubled; g is similar, shifting to *k* only in some dialects, although when doubled it appears as *ck, kk; d* shifts to *t* in most dialects, although here it must be remembered that the so-called West Germanic dialects had the sound *th-* (still visible in many cognate English words), which changed during the Old High German period to *d.* Thus Old and indeed modern High German show *d* in the definite article (*die*) where English has *th* (*the*).

This is, of course, a great oversimplification of the sound shift. It seems to have begun in the south, and to have spread to the northwest. Not all the relevant sounds were affected at the same time or to the same extent geographically. Although scholars have recently found very early evidence of shifted forms in the Rhineland,[6] Bavarian, Alemannic, and Lombardic seem to have been affected first, and the first two show the most extensive spread of the changes. Lombardic is only preserved in a very few documents, and was soon abandoned as a living Germanic language, but Bavarian and Alemannic are customarily grouped together as the Upper German representatives of Old High German, distinguishing them from the various Frankish, or Franconian, dialects.

Closest of these to Upper German are East Franconian (centering on Würzburg, Erlangen, and the Main) and Rhenish Franconian (extending from Hessen through Worms to a border with Alemannic just below Karlsruhe). The region of the Rhenish Franconian area closest to Alemannic territory is where the South Rhenish Franconian dialect was spoken, a dialect that is well recorded in the work of Otfrid. Furthest away from Upper German, and least affected by the sound shift, are the central Franconian dialects, the Old High German used in the region of Trier— known as Moselle Franconian—and of Cologne—known as Ripuarian Franconian. It may be noted that one Franconian dialect was unaffected by the shift: Low Franconian, in the area of what are now the Low Countries, and attested in early documents as one of the two principal continental Old Low German dialects, the other being Old Saxon.

The Upper German and most of the Franconian dialects, then, are High German in that they show at least some evidence of the shifts. In fact, all of them show at least two specific changes. That of *k,* single after a vowel, shifted to *h* (written later as *ch*), is still visible in German *machen,* English *make.* That of *t,* when initial, doubled, or after a consonant, shifted to *z* (*ts*), is still apparent in the German words *zehn, sitzen,* and *Herz* against English *ten, sit* (*sittan* in Anglo-Saxon), and *heart.* The shift cannot be dated with complete accuracy, and when German appears in writing in the eighth century, many of the changes are already evident. But onomastic evidence—the datable names of people and places—leads to the conclusion that it probably began around 500.

There still remains, however, a very considerable variation among the different dialects of High German, especially between the extreme Franconian and Upper German ones. Even when geographically close, however, divergences are striking. Here are two translations of part of the Apostle's Creed, one in Alemannic and one in South Rhenish Franconian. The text reads: "I believe in God the Father almighty, maker of heaven and earth: And in Jesus Christ his only son, our Lord, who was conceived by the Holy Ghost, born of the Virgin Mary, suffered under Pontius Pilate, was crucified, died, and was buried. He descended into hell; the third day he rose again from the dead. He ascended into heaven and sitteth at the right hand of God the Father almighty; from thence he shall come to judge the quick and the dead." The first German version, from St. Gallen in Switzerland, reads (MSD LVII, St. V, Lb. VI/2):

Kilaubu in kot fater almahticun, kiscaft himiles enti erda. enti in Ihesum Christ, sun sinan ainacun, unseran truhtin, der inphangan ist fona uuihemu keiste, kiporan fona Mariun macadi euuikeru, kimartrot in kiuualtiu Pilates, in cruce pislacan, tot enti picrapan, stehic in uuizzi, in drittin take erstoont fona totem, stehic in himil, sizit az zesuun cotes fateres almahtikin, dhana chuumftic ist sonen qhuekhe enti tote. . . .

The second is from Weissenburg (MSD LVI, St. VI, Lb. XIIIc):

Gilaubiu in got fater almahtigon, scepphion himiles enti erda. Endi in heilen-ton Christ, suno sinan einagon, truhtin unseran. Ther infanganer ist fona heiligemo geiste, giboran fona Mariun magadi, giuuizzinot bi pontisgen Pilate, In cruci bislagan, toot endi bigraban. Nidhar steig ci helliu, in thritten dage arstuat fona tóotem. Úf steig ci himilom, gisaaz ci cesuun gotes fateres al-mahtiges, thanan quẹmendi ci ardeilenne quecchem endi dóodem. . . .

Variations in vocabulary need not concern us yet (although some are apparent in the passages quoted). What is striking is the orthographic divergence between the two texts, and indeed even within a single text (see the treatment of *toot/dood,* "dead," in the second). The Alemannic text, too, spells the word for God either with an initial *c* or a *k,* and the rendering of the *z/ts* sound was plainly a problem, too. But for the distinction between High and Low German, both versions show *h* (*ch*) and *z/ts* against Low German *k* and *t.* English *quick* (as opposed to "dead") has its final sound shown as -*ch* in one text, and, even more extreme, as -*kh* in the other; and English *to* and *at* are represented by *ci* in the Franconian text and *az* in the Alemannic, respectively. Between the two dialects as representative of different forms of High German we may note the shifting of *b* to *p* and *g* to *k,* both typical Upper German features, in the Alemannic text (*kot* against *got, kiporan* against *giboran*).

Even to speak of the separate dialects in Old High German writings can be misleading. Within a single small text, features of quite different dialects may appear. An early prayer (MSD LVIII, St. XI, Lb. XIV) begins: "Truhtin god, thu mir hilp indi forgip mir gauuitzi" ("Lord God, grant me help and give me understanding"), in which *god* is Franconian and *hilp* points to an area not far from Low German. *Truhtin* and *forgip* could be Upper German, however. Possibly the text was copied from an original in one dialect by a scribe whose native dialect was different. The situation is not unusual. Old High German is a dead language, studied on the basis of written documents originating in a number of monastic centers. These centers were able to impose only a certain degree of regularity on the documents they produced, and there is no consistency.

It might have been expected that some attempt to impose conformity might come from the Frankish ruling class. The kings of the Franks did indeed show some interest in their own language even in Merovingian times, and Chilperic, who ruled from 561 to 584, added four letters to the Latin alphabet, presumably to facilitate the writing of Germanic words (although also probably in imitation of what the Roman writer Suetonius had to say about the efforts of the emperor Claudius to improve Latin orthography).[7] Charlemagne and his successor, Lewis the Pious, may have seen some attempt at standardization toward Franconian forms even outside the dialect area, but this is unlikely to have been extensive.[8] A separate problem is raised here by the question of "West Franconian." German-language documents appear in what is now France even after the general adoption of the local Romance language, and there has been some speculation on the possibility of a Franconian language maintained in the Carolingian court. Evidence for this remains slight, however, and the problem is complex.[9]

Even the meaning of the word "German" is questionable. The Latin word *theodiscus,* although a Germanic borrowing, can refer to any High or Low German dialect: Charlemagne uses it for Saxon and for Bavarian, and Otfrid, who uses it in Latin, avoids it in German. Only in the eleventh century does it appear, as *diutisch (deutsch*) with a general meaning.[10] At the period with which we are concerned, the terms "language" and "dialect" lack precision. The Old High German "language"—which never existed as a unity—is the sum of a series of tribal vernaculars, related to one another, and sharing at least some of a sequence of sound-changes not found in other "West Germanic" vernaculars, although they do have features in common with them which are not found in the North Germanic languages, or in what survive of the East Germanic.

The Literature

The largest question-mark has always accompanied the word "literature" when applied to the Old High German period. Otfrid's poem on Christ is a selfconscious work of art, but many of the remaining examples of Old High German poetry, even, have been written on occasional blank leaves or in the margins of Latin manuscripts. A different consideration arises with the prose. While we do not, for the most part, have to reckon here with accidental survivals, virtually everything we have is translated from Latin, and a good deal of that consists of single-word glosses rather than continuous prose.

The major anthologies of Old High German at the end of the last century tended to avoid the word "literature" altogether. Karl Müllenhoff and Wilhelm Scherer entitled their collection *"Denkmäler* deutscher Poesie und Prosa,"* [*Monuments* of German poetry and prose], while Elias von Steinmeyer took this further and referred to them as *Sprachdenkmäler* [Linguistic monuments]. The other side of the coin, however, was represented by scholars like Eduard Sievers on the one hand, who, preoccupied with a metrical theory, saw as poetry many works which plainly are not. Rudolf Koegel, on the other hand, devoted an entire volume of a literary history to works that may have existed as part of a general Germanic oral tradition, but are simply not extant.[11]

However useful the neutral word "monument" may be, we may still seek and find art in Old High German poetry, and with the prose we may note the emergence of a potentially literary language and the development, even in such apparently restricted sources as the glosses, of a new and complex philosophical vocabulary. Most of that vocabulary, however, is linked with a specific set of ideas, with Christianity. With a few exceptions, the history of the Old High German writings is completely bound up with the Christian church.

Christian missionary activity had affected Germany since Merovingian times.[12] The earliest monks seem to have been Irish. St. Columban founded the monastery of Bobbio in northern Italy in 612, and his disciple Gall that at St. Gallen shortly afterwards. Irish influence continued in the south, and we can observe Irish influence on the language at various points. With the rise of the Carolingians is associated a later, Anglo-Saxon mission, which consolidated Christianity in some areas, and brought it to others. The activities of St. Boniface and St. Willibrord, both Anglo-Saxons, are the most notable, and they founded monasteries at Echternach, near Trier, and at Fulda—two vital centers for Old High German. Later still, Charlemagne brought scholars like Alcuin of York to his palace school. The newly formed monasteries developed, and produced their own major Latin scholars, like Hrabanus Maurus of Fulda.

Monastic centers became the focus not only for renewed missionary activity and for Latin learning, but also for the earliest use of German. Bavarian religious houses included those at Freising, Wessobrunn, Regensburg (St. Emmeram), and Mon(d)see; in the Alemannic area were those at St. Gallen, and on the island of Reichenau in Lake Constance. For South Rhenish Franconian we have referred already to Otfrid's monastery at Weissenburg, and in the Rhenish Franconian dialect area proper were Lorsch, Worms, and the diocesan center, Mainz. The chief East Franconian monasteries were at Fulda, Würzburg, and Ebersberg (although the latter are in present-day Bavaria), and Central Franconian centers were at Trier, Cologne, and Echternach.[13] Even with the reservations regarding dialect unity noted above, the association of a particular monastery with the local dialect is not straightforward. The Reichenau was an imperial Frankish foundation, for example, and drew upon Frankish families for many of its monks.

Reading the Texts

A variety of problems quite unfamiliar to those concerned with the writings of later periods arise with the study of Old High German. The sometimes entirely fortuitous survival of the small body of writing means that texts are fragmentary, damaged, and difficult to read. In some cases, indeed, they are simply nonexistent: that is, we are sometimes aware that a work known to us in Latin had a German original which is lost. A metrical life of St. Gall, for example, written in German, was translated about a century and a half after its composition, into Latin, a language which the translator—who tells us so in a preface—found less barbaric. The German is lost, now. Other Latin texts point fairly clearly to lost originals, even if we are less certain that they existed. An epic poem, known in Latin by the title *Waltharius,* has an Anglo-Saxon vernacular counterpart and probably had a German one. In the case of some smaller Latin pieces which look as if they were translations of German originals, those originals have sometimes even been "reconstructed" and the results included as genuine in anthologies.

The chance survival of very many of the texts leads to yet more potential problems. To take an extreme example, one quatrain has come down to us only because a sixteenth-century map-maker copied it, without any knowledge of what it was, from a stone inscription, to use in a decorative border. Even in less complex transmissions we may have to come to terms with badly worn or damaged manuscripts, in addition to the possibility of erratic copying, of possibly corrupt originals, or of confusion between dialects. Some texts use codes and ciphers; some are simply incomprehensible. In some cases, too, special arguments have to be made to determine whether the text is Old High German at all, and in at least one case there is still doubt as to whether a text is a forgery or not. Often the editorial efforts of the last century have not helped. A mixed Latin and German poem about a nun and her male admirer has suffered twice: once by erasure for moral reasons in the Middle Ages and then again in the nineteenth century when editors used chemicals to try and bring out the lost words, damaging the manuscript further.

It is important to remember that we are dealing with a manuscript-based literature, and that the uniformity and conventions imposed by the printed book are far in the unimaginable future. Consultation *only* of editions—or worse, of translations—can be very misleading, and efforts should always be made to consult the manuscripts. Photo-facsimiles of the major texts, at least, are readily available. The problem may be demonstrated by an example. Horst Dieter Schlosser's Old High German anthology is a parallel text. On the right-hand page he prints the following version of the opening of an early charm: "Phol und Wodan ritten in den Wald. Da verrenkte sich Balders Fohlen seinen Fuß. Da besprach ihn Sindgund (und) Sunna, ihre Schwester, da besprach ihn Frija (und) Volla, ihre Schwester, da besprach ihn Wodan, so gut wie (nur) er es konnte. . ."[14] ("Phol and Wodan were riding in the wood. Balder's horse sprained its foot. Then Sindgund (and) Sunna, her sister, conjured it, then Frija (and) Volla, her sister conjured it, then Wodan conjured it, as well as (only) he knew how. . ."). Details of the translation are not at issue here, but the insertion of the conjunctions might, in fact, add a pair of pagan goddesses not necessarily present in the original, since Sunna and Volla may stand in simple apposition—"Sindgund, the sister of Sunna."

The Old High German text on the left-hand page has an orderly look, set out as verse, with the names capitalized. Schlosser does, it is true, italicize the *th* in the Old High German form of Sindgund, *Sinthgunt,* and the *h* in the first word, but not every edition does so. The original, however, has no capitals at all, apart from the very first letter, and it is doubtful whether *Phol* and *Balder* are even names at all. Sindgund appears in the manuscript as *sinhtgunt,* and *Phol* is written as *Pol,* with an *h* added, perhaps as an afterthought, over the *o.* Nor is the original laid out as verse, but as continuous prose, and the punctuation is, of course, editorial. The decisions of the various editors of the Old High German texts are not, of course, capricious. They are based on a striving for intelligibility, and take into account comparable forms and names in other works. But much does remain speculative, and the editorial apparatus must neither be forgotten nor accepted without question.

Two problems have to be borne in mind, one proper to the modern reader, the other that of the (usually) anonymous early medieval writer. It is sometimes very difficult indeed for the modern reader to establish with certainty what a text means. The *hapax legomenon* chosen editorially as the title of the apocalyptic poem *Muspilli* is still unclear. But the difficulties for the writers of Old High German were also considerable. Committing sounds to writing without precedent and finding words for new concepts in large numbers are problems all too easily forgotten in a literate society. As regards the first problem, the Latin alphabet is not ideally suited to German, and indeed, alternatives have been used: the Goths used for their Germanic language a modified Greek alphabet, and the runic letters were used in the earliest stages of German. Additional runic-inspired letters to represent the sounds *w* and *th* were used in writing, following Anglo-Saxon practice, in some early manuscripts, but these did not persist. For the vocabulary, the expression of Christian ideas in the vernacular necessitated the provision of a whole range of new abstracts. An illustration of the problem is provided by the fact that the Old High German word *bifahan* (*befangen,* "include," "surround," etc.) is used to gloss thirty-three different Latin words.[15]

The limited number of surviving works in Old High German makes their arrangement in the form of a literary history difficult. The literary language of the period in which these works were written is not German, but Latin, and the German works declare themselves to be less important, either by the manner of their survival or indeed *expressis verbis*: Otfrid speaks of the "unpolished rusticity" of German against Latin. Yet to place the German works into the historicocultural context of the Latin Middle Ages would be to swallow them up completely. It is the job of the critic to assess these limited survivals for themselves as the small beginnings of a literature and a literary language, while remaining conscious of their relative importance in their own time.

The development toward a broad vernacular literature, and toward the possibility of a genuine literary prose, is erratic, but some lines of continuity may be drawn. The processes of translation continue right through the period and beyond, and so does the quite separate tradition of vernacular glossing. Some genres—the charms are the best example—are also continuous in themselves. There is, finally, one unifying framework for all of Old High German literature, and that is the Christian church. Even within the limited corpus of writings in Old High German, pre-Christian material is very limited indeed, and what texts there are owe their survival to monastic efforts. The rest depends upon, and to a large extent was written, in the service of the Christian church, and it is within that context that the cultural importance and, indeed, the aesthetic value of the writings in the emergent German language must be assessed.

Chapter Two
Functional Prose for State and Church
The Earliest Inscriptions

The first evidence of writing in High German—perhaps coincident with the sound shift—is not found in documents, but in inscriptions. About sixty examples are known of the southern Germanic runic survivals, messages that employ the runic alphabet, an angular set of characters suitable for carving, used by most of the Germanic tribes. The runic letters seem to have had a ritual significance of their own. In southwestern Europe they are found scratched, often crudely, on the back of brooches and other small artifacts, primarily of the sixth or seventh centuries. Sometimes they appear on swords and other weapons. Most of the inscriptions contain just names or the alphabet itself, although longer pieces are known. The brooches are usually found in female graves in the Alemannic area, and the names inscribed presumably refer to the owners or to the givers of the brooches, and two names are often found together. Of the fuller texts, a disc brooch from Bülach, near Zurich, has the words "husband, embrace me," and a bow brooch from near Augsburg demands special attention as containing not only personal names but the mythological ones Wodan and Donar. Both are from the early seventh century. A slightly later disc brooch from near Worms, however, is clearly Christian, although its inscription, "God fura dih deofile," may be interpreted either as "God before you, devil," or "God protect you, Theophilus." While these inscriptions provide some evidence of the use of formulaic phrases at an early stage, most of them are private inscriptions, for the purposes of the named person or the owner. One inscription found on a stone may have been public, but it contains only names.[1]

The runic alphabet is not used in manuscripts in Germany. It is, however, quoted in a Latin encyclopedic work in a ninth-century manuscript from St. Gallen, together with other alphabets. The *Abecedarium Nordmannicum* (MSD V) follows the runes themselves with a mnemonic verse built up on the names of the individual runes, which also stood for whole words. Thus the first two runes, *f* and *u,* are named *feu* ("beast," German *Vieh*) and *ur* ("aurochs"), and the whole verse has an incantatory effect. The text as a whole, however, is virtually impossible to interpret. Gerhard Eis comments that "pretty well everything is uncertain: age, decipherment, script, language, verse-form, and most of all the content."[2] Whether it belongs at all in a survey of Old High German is a matter of debate.

Vernacular inscriptions using the Roman alphabet are, on the other hand, rare. A gravestone, carved with figures and found at Bingen (St. LXXXV, Lb. IV/2), bears the epitaph "Remember Diederich, the son of Go(defrid) and Drulind." The second name could in fact be any similar compound.[3] Beyond this we find, on coins, for example, only personal names; on the coinage, too, the rest of the inscription copied Roman or Byzantine models—and so, frequently, did the portraits.

Legal Texts

Although the Church must have been instrumental in the preservation of relevant documents, as it was for the exclusive use of the Roman alphabet, the earliest evidence of a genuinely public use of German belongs in the realm of social administration. Legal documents in Old High German are found over a period of several centuries, but they may be considered together at this point.

Individual German words are found, first of all, in the various legal codes of the Germanic tribes, and one such code was translated more fully. As far as the occurrence of single words is concerned, we are not dealing here with glosses, German equivalents provided for Latin words in a Latin context, but with the reverse: the German words are usually the original names for specific crimes, which are then paraphrased in Latin, the language in which the codes are ultimately preserved.

One should not, in fact, speak of legal codes in this period. We are concerned with collections of customs rather than with a statutory system. The documents are, however, of considerable social and linguistic importance.[4] A large number of these legal compilations have survived from the fifth century onward. Those of the eastern tribes are the earliest—the laws of the Burgundians and the Goths—although these are not relevant here. Of special significance to the study of the western tribes, however, both

High and Low German, are two slightly later collections: the law of the Salian Franks, and the Lombardic *Edict of Rothar.* The latter, dating from 643, was written down about fifty years later and revised on subsequent occasions. It is our major source for the Lombardic language, providing us with words like *uuer-gild* ("wergild"), recompense paid for crimes against a person. The laws themselves are of some interest: one imposes a heavy fine on a man who refers in anger to another man as a coward, and proscriptions against accusing women of witchcraft or vampirism give an idea of contemporary beliefs.

The law of the Salian Franks, the *Lex Salica,* is older, begun perhaps in the sixth century in the time of King Clovis (481–511), but extensively revised and adapted over the years. The oldest version has sixty-five headings, and by the eighth century this had increased to one hundred, being reduced again in the ninth to seventy. Some of the paragraphs have been far-reaching: the Salic ban (in the 100-title text) on female inheritance of land when any possible male heir survives precluded Queen Victoria, on her accession to the English throne in 1837, from assuming the sovereignity of Hanover.

The *Lex Salica* seems to have influenced similar collections, such as those of the Ripuarian Franks (*Lex Ribuaria*), the Bavarians (*Lex Baiuuariorum*), and the Alemannic tribes (*Lex Alamannorum*) in the seventh and eighth centuries, and the rather later *Lex Frisionum* of the Frisians, as well as the laws of the Saxons, Angles, and other tribes. Many contain Germanic legal expressions, usually preceded by formulas like "quod dicunt Baiuuarii" ("as the Bavarians say") and the like.

The Germanic portions of the *Lex Salica* are difficult in the earliest manuscripts, eighth-century versions of the 100-title text. Germanic words are frequently preceded by the term, often abbreviated, *Malloberg.* This has been taken to mean "council hill," and to imply "tribal legal term" by extension from the place of judgment. The words themselves, which are probably Low Franconian, a Low German dialect, are very difficult to interpret, and were probably not understood by the scribes. Far clearer is a later version of the Salian laws, although it provides no help with the interpretation of the erroneously named *Malberg* or *Malloberg Glosses.* A small part survives of a translation into east Franconian, a High German dialect, of the seventy-title text. The language is of the early ninth century, and the manuscript from Fulda, and what survives is an incomplete list of the headings, and part of the two first paragraphs (MSD LXV, St. X, Lb. XVIII). One of the paragraphs concerned deals with the theft of pigs and gives details of the recompense due to the injured parties.

Several more specific legal documents are known from the Old High German period. These include brief records of land gifts to churches and monasteries, and frequently contain little more than names (Lb. II/1–2 etc.). More complex are the official documents known as *Markbeschreibungen* ("boundary-charters"), of which we have two full examples. One, referring to Hammelburg, in Bavaria, records a donation of land there to the monastery of Fulda (MSD LXIII, St. XII, Lb. II/3) in 777. Various names are given, and the description of the land itself is in a mixture of German and Latin. Very similar is a document from Würzburg, but this describes the town boundaries (MSD LXIV, St. XXIV, Lb. II/4). It dates from 779, and notes church properties in the area. The manuscript version—which was written in the late tenth century—contains two texts. The first begins in Latin and then falls into the mixed pattern of the Hammelburg document. The second is entirely in German, and it has been suggested that this was intended as a public notice. The area described is not quite the same, however, and the witness names are also different.

Brief mention may be made of the *Heberollen,* records of monastic income from tributary-liable communities. These have survived only in Low German, from Essen (MSD LXIX), Freckenhorst, and Werden. Special attention must be paid, on the other hand, to two High German documents of considerable historical importance: the record of a political treaty and a Carolingian charter in German.

Given the Frankish system of divided land-inheritance, the empire of Charlemagne was split up, after the death of his son, Lewis the Pious, among his three grandsons: Charles, king of the western lands, of France; Lewis II as king of the eastern parts, of Germany; and Lothar, the nominal emperor, as ruler of territories between the two—Lotharingia, modern Lorraine. The brothers fought among themselves, and in 842 Charles and Lewis swore a treaty of alliance and mutual help: should one of them be at war with Lothar, the other would offer no aid to the emperor. The situation at which the treaty was concluded is described in a Latin history. Charles and Lewis met with their armies at Strasbourg and swore the oath. Lewis used the *lingua romana*—Old French—so that Charles's army would understand him, and Charles swore in German. Then the two armies swore a similar oath, this time in their own languages. The description of the swearing of the *Strasbourg Oaths* (MSD LXVII, St. XV, Lb. XXI/1) was written down in the tenth century, and the scribe seems to have understood French, but not the Rhenish Franconian of the German oath. Thus he wrote lines like "in dimit luheren innohhein iut hing nege ganga," which illustrates a familiar difficulty with Old High German—establishing the text. Those words should read: "indi mit Lu(d)heren in nohheiniu thing ne geganga. . ." ("and unite with Lothar in no common cause. . .").[5] The swearing in two languages brings home to us the linguistic division in Charlemagne's empire fairly soon after his death.

A capitulary is an official ordinance (divided into chapters) issued by a ruler, which can amend tribal laws. Usually it deals with the administration of public and church matters, and one such decree, made in 818 by Lewis the Pious, was put into Middle Franconian, perhaps in the tenth century. The manuscript has been lost, and the *Trierer Capitulare* [Trier Capitulary] is known from a copy published in 1626 (MSD LXVI, St. XL, Lb. XIX). The German is not a translation, but rather a word-for-word glossing of the Latin original, which is concerned with the laws of inheritance. The capitulary makes the point that a man may dispose of his belongings as he likes, and calls for notarized gifts (with witnesses from the same tribe), be these to relatives or to the Church, so that later disputes (arising from tribal blood-laws) may be avoided. We do not know why the translation/glossing was carried out over a century after the decree. Possibly it was used in a private legal case, conceivably one concerning church property, in support of long-standing precedent.[6]

Creeds, Paternosters, and Confessions

As might be expected, considerable effort was devoted early in the Old High German period, and continuing right through, to the adapting into German of basic Christian texts—the Lord's Prayer, the Creed, baptismal professions of faith, and more extended catechetical pieces. The need to make clear to the people the central beliefs of the Church is underlined in a number of official pronouncements from the time of Charlemagne. The best known is a capitulary of 23 March 789 known as the *Admonitio Generalis* [General Precept], which calls in Chapter 70 for the Lord's Prayer to be taught and explained, and the Gloria and the Sanctus to be sung. Later documents, issued from church synods in the early ninth century, reinforce this, and the Synod of Frankfurt in June 794 laid down that "no one should believe that God is to be worshiped in three languages only, for God is to be adored in all languages. . . ." Later capitularies call for the memorizing and testing of the Lord's Prayer and the Creed.[7]

The matter of translation was no light one. Christianity was a relatively recent faith in Germany and contained new and difficult concepts. The German language, only now being committed to writing, had at the same time to find a vocabulary for complex metaphysical ideas. However this vocabulary was created, problems could arise. If a loan-word technique was used—if the Latin word was simply made into a German one—the idea as such, if not at least linked with something concrete, could well remain obscure. Thus to render the Latin word *evangelium* ("gospel") as *evangelio* might not be particularly helpful. Indeed, alternatives were offered for that word. If, however, the various elements in a Latin word are rendered literally, providing us with a new compound, the artificiality might still lead to difficulties. To render *con-scientia* ("conscience") as *ga-wizzani*—this technique is known as loan-translation—may retain the idea of knowledge (modern German *wissen*) in the new word, but the spiritual implications are hardly clear. Finally, even semantic borrowing could be dangerous. This method grafts the new, Christian, ideas onto words already in existence. If the word used is a secular one, then the religious meaning may be obscured, at least for a time. The word *truhtin* ("lord"), applied to Christ, probably retained for a long time overtones of the warrior-leader meaning it had originally. Giving a new meaning to a word with pagan religious significance has a similar danger: that the pagan sense may survive. Even now, a child, aware of the word "ghost" meaning "spook," may be confused by the phrase "Holy Ghost" as an equivalent for *sanctus spiritus*. [8]

In spite of the comments of the Frankfurt Synod, Latin still remained one of the three sacred languages, and as such, the very syntax of Latin liturgical formulations acquired a kind of sanctity. In German, then, what looks like a wooden and literal translation may equally well be an intentioned adherence to the original form. The problem of what constitutes "good" Old High German is very difficult, as is the whole issue of freedom or slavishness in a translation. Official pronouncements such as the *Admonitio Generalis* must not, however, be overemphasized. They do give an indication of encouragement, but the Old High German texts we possess need not be seen as evidence for a programmatic policy. Heinz Rupp reminds us that "with all these functional texts one must ask oneself whether they were not composed more or less *ad hoc* from Latin formulas at hand, for use on the spot."[9] Some of our texts may even predate the *Admonitio*. One final point is that the Latin texts themselves, even biblical ones, may vary, in addition to which a translator might be working from a damaged or abbreviated original. A proper appreciation of the emergence of the German language in these texts depends on an awareness of the variety of problems that had to be faced.

Of the baptismal vows, the most interesting is a Low German one, in Old Saxon (MSD LI, St. III, Lb. XVI/2/ii), which may be connected with Charlemagne's campaigns. The text calls upon the catechumen to forsake the devil with the words "I forsake all the devil's works and words, Thunaer and Woden and Saxnot and all the wicked ones who go with them. . . ." A profession of belief in the Trinity follows. A Franconian text (MSD LII, St. IV, Lb. XVI/1) from the same manuscript as the *Merseburg Charms* (see Chapter 4), and perhaps originally from Fulda, calls for a renunciation only of "the gods of the heathens," but includes the Church, the forgiveness of sins, and life after death in the profession of belief. A parallel fragment of this text has survived in a later manuscript (MSD LIII).

A consideration of the various versions of the Lord's Prayer can be illuminating.[10] It is necessary first, however, to comment briefly on the Latin text (Matthew 6:9–13, cited, and Luke 11:2–4).

[9]Pater noster qui es in caelis, sanctificetur nomen tuum, [10]adveniat regnum tuum, fiat voluntas tua sicut in caelo et in terra, [11]Panem nostrum super-substantialem da nobis hodie, [12]et dimitte nobis debita nostra, sicut et nos dimittimus debitoribus nostris, [13]et ne nos inducas in tentationem sed libera nos a malo.

This is the form authorized at present, and the verse-numbers are also modern. The opening words give the prayer a title, and this fixes the Latin order of noun plus adjective. In the same verse *in caelis* ("in heaven") is a plural, but the equivalent in the next verse is singular. The relative clause in verse 9 has a third-person pronoun (*qui*) and a second-person verb (*es*). *Sanctificetur* ("hallowed be") is of course a passive, and the Latin possessive pronouns regularly follow the noun. In verse 11 the word *supersubstantialem* ("supersubstantial") is found in many early versions as *cotidianum* ("daily"). Finally the imperative "lead us not" is rendered as a subjunctive verb, as Latin has no negative imperative. "Deliver us. . ." is a regular imperative. All these points need consideration when examining the German texts.

Probably the oldest text is the *St. Gallen Paternoster and Creed* (MSD LVII, St. V, Lb. VI), an eighth-century version. The two opening words are in the Latin order, but the prayer is still known as the *Vaterunser,* so this is not significant. The relative clause is avoided in favor of a straight "thou art in heaven," and the plural *caelis* is rendered as a singular. Otherwise the

Latin word-order is closely followed, in phrases like *prooth unseer emezzihic* ("bread our continual"). In the "lead us not" clause, the word-order is followed, but a regular imperative is used. One signal error occurs. For the passive "hallowed be" the translator uses *uuihi,* the imperative "hallow." In spite of attempts to justify this, it still looks like a simple (but theologically vital) error, probably because the original was abbreviated, the verbal ending represented as a flourish of the pen. There are errors in the Creed, too, as when the word *Pontio ("Pontius"* [Pilate]) is translated as if it were *potentia* ("power").[11]

A ninth-century Rhenish Franconian Lord's Prayer in the *Weissenburg Catechism* (MSD LVI, St. VI, Lb. XIII) adopts a similar translation for the *qui es* clause, but distinguishes between the plural and singular form of "in heaven." The passive "hallowed be" is rendered correctly as *giuuihit si* (a later, Alemannic text has *uuerdo geheiligot,* incidentally, which shows how the vocabulary may vary). A more or less contemporary Bavarian text from Freising, which exists in two manuscripts (MSD LV, St. VIII, Lb. XII), offers a translation and commentary of the Paternoster. Even these two parallel manuscripts have some divergences in the translation. The first (and earlier) text renders the opening relative clause as *du pist* ("thou art"), the second as a third-person clause proper, *der ist* ("who is"). Both have the first "in heaven" in its plural form, however. For "thy name" the first text has *namo din,* the second *din namo,* but the position is reversed with "thy will." In both cases, "thy kingdom" is placed in the Latin order. The word "bread" in this text is, however, rendered *pilipi* ("nourishment"), which is presumably a deliberate attempt to get away from a literal reading of the passage, to make the commentary somewhat easier.

Both the Freising text and the *Weissenburg Catechism* go beyond the level of simple translation. Both contain commentaries explaining the prayer, and the Weissenburg collection contains too a list of sins, a version of the Apostles' Creed, then—rather unusually—a translation of the Athanasian Creed, and finally a doxology. There is some evidence that the scribe was combining the work of different translators and making some coordinating adjustments. The whole is certainly in the spirit of the *Admonitio,* even if the precise circumstances of its writing remain unknown.

The tradition of the Old High German Confessions, *Beichten,* which appear, often together with a version of the Creed, after the ninth century, is again a highly diversified one. These Confessions are essentially lists of sins (potentially) committed, which could have been read out as a public statement during a service, or made in private to a priest, or used as a kind of reference either by the priest or the penitent. A large number are known from all the dialects, and they continue to appear throughout the Middle Ages (MSD LXXII–LXXVIIIa, St. XLI–LI, Lb. XXII/1–5). Some of the earlier Confessions are linked with one another, and Georg Baesecke, in an extended study published in 1925, tried to derive them all from a single archetype, which he reconstructed, seeing this in its turn as a direct result of the *Admonitio*.[12] He saw the monasteries of Fulda and Lorsch as the starting points. This notion of "planned duplication and dissemination" is no longer felt to be valid, as many of the relationships are tenuous: one returns to the concept of *ad hoc* preparation of material from sources that can no longer be traced.

Among the earliest versions are the *Saxon Confession,* a Low German text found in the manuscript of a Latin Confession (MSD LXXII, St. XLV, Lb. XXII/5), and in High German those from Fulda (MSD LXXIII, St. XLVIII) and Lorsch (MSD LXXIIb, St. XLVI, Lb. XXII/2), as well as the oldest of a group from Bavaria, one from St. Emmeram in Regensburg (MSD LXXVIIIa, St. XLI, Lb XXII/1a). The texts vary in length, but most begin with the general formula: "Lord, I confess all my sins and misdeeds, all that I have spoken, done or thought evil, words, works and thoughts, remembered or unremembered, knowingly and unknowingly. . ." and go on to enumerate the specific sins. The social and linguistic importance of these texts is clear. The *Lorsch Confession,* for example, lists lasciviousness, sloth, murder, manslaughter, and greed, as well as the failure to keep the other commandments. This is a normal penitential sequence, but the same text also includes a reference to not paying tithes. The *Würzburg Confesion* (MSD LXXVI, St. XLIV) includes both lust and unnatural sexual behavior (*uncusgimo site sodomitico*). The Bavarian Confession from St. Emmeram is of special interest, in that it has a parallel text (known in two manuscripts) which adds to the penitential section a prose prayer soliciting divine help in being able to serve God: the *St. Emmeram Prayer* (MSD LXXVIIIb, St. XLII, Lb. XXII/1b). Curiously, a version of this prayer is also found in Old Church Slavonic.[13]

Confessions that have appended to them a translation of the Creed usually contain other liturgical material as well (MSD LXXVII–XCVI, St. XXVIII and LII–LX). One example must suffice as illustration of this. The *Third Benediktbeuren Confession* (MSD XCVI, St. LX), from the very end of our period, includes a Creed, an admonition from the priest, an exhortation to confession, the penitential passage itself, which opens with a vow rejecting the devil, then a postconfessional prayer. Earlier Confessions sometimes ended with an absolution, and this appears here in Latin and in German, followed by a final admonition, and a prayer for the Church.

Of these extended catechetical texts, the *Bamberg* and the *First Wesso-brunn Confessions* are worthy of note (MSD XC–XCI, St. XXVIII). The two texts, in manuscripts of the eleventh and twelfth centuries, are parallel, and contain the usual thesaurus of sins. The Bamberg version, in East Franconian, is longer than the Bavarian text from Wessobrunn, but that version seems to have been adapted for the use of women—some of the pronominal adjectives applied to the speaker are feminine.

The length of these and similar texts seems to bespeak their use as *Beichtspiegel,* as confessional handbooks, rather than as parts of the liturgy proper. The precise liturgical position of two other religious texts is less clear, however. The so-called *Frankish Prayer* (MSD LVIII, St. XI, Lb. XIV) belongs probably to the first years of the ninth century, and simply calls upon God for help and grace. The language shows clear features both of Rhenish Franconian and of Bavarian, but it is assumed—and the case is not untypical—that the original was Frankish, copied by a Bavarian scribe. Interest is added to the piece, which is built up of well-known Latin liturgical formulas, by the fact that it appears in a manuscript with the *Admonitio Generalis,* and may be a direct response to it. A further curiosity is that the German prayer is followed by a translation into Latin, and that the German came first is indicated in the use there of a dative with the verb "to help," which is a German but not a Latin grammatical feature. The *Exhortatio ad plebem Christianum* [Exhortation to Christian People] (MSD LIV, St. IX, Lb. X), known in two manuscripts, is a kind of sermon, probably intended for the baptismal service. The instructions for godparents that it contains reflect a capitulary of 802, and the last part refers to the learning of the Lord's Prayer, recalling again the Carolingian efforts to aid Christinaity on an official basis. The text is a word-for-word rendering of the Latin original.

A slightly later small piece may conclude this survey of functional prose. The *Bavarian Ordination Oath* (MSD LXVIII, St. XIII, Lb. XXI/2) is for the priest to swear to the bishop, much as a secular vassal might. Oaths of this kind were introduced during the ninth century, and the language of the text points also to that period.[14]

Chapter Three
Glosses and Translations

Between 1879 and 1922 Eduard Sievers and Elias von Steinmeyer published five volumes of collected glosses in Old High German, and glosses have continued to be discovered and published with some regularity ever since. The glosses are important to the study of Old High German for a variety of reasons, and they represent the most basic stage in the emergence of a complex literary language. We can, in fact, draw a fairly clear schematic line from single-word glosses to complete interlinear versions of Latin works, to various types of translations proper. Such a scheme, however, must not be taken as a chronological line of development. The earliest glosses are probably more or less contemporary with functional translations of fundamental Christian texts, and the work of glossing Latin texts goes on throughout the period and beyond. It is convenient to look first at glosses and then at translations, but it must be borne in mind that we are dealing with parallel developments.

Glosses

In our context, glosses are German words written as equivalents to specific Latin words or phrases in manuscripts of Latin texts. In a wider sense, a gloss can be any word or phrase added either by way of translation, expansion, or explanation, and a Latin manuscript can of course be glossed with Latin words. These are sometimes found side by side with German additions. In the manuscripts with which we are concerned, the German word—the *interpretamentum* of the Latin *lemma*—may be written above or below the Latin word, as an interlinear gloss. It may appear in the margin, as a marginal gloss. If the manuscript with the glosses is then recopied, the German words may be transcribed following the Latin words to which they refer. In this case the glosses are termed context glosses.

It is important to remember that the German glosses depend on the Latin text. Even where the Latin original is itself a dictionary (of Greek and

Latin, say), or is akin to a thesaurus or synonym-list, the German words will still depend on the Latin layout. Sometimes, it is true, the German words are gathered afterwards, and arranged, sometimes alphabetically, at the end of a Latin text, making what is properly termed a glossary. Normally, however, glosses are found in the text itself. That text can be sporadically or fully glossed. A manuscript of II Corinthians, for example, preserved in the St. Gallen Codex 70, has only occasional German words (Ahd. Gl. I, 765f.); a sixth-century Gospel from St. Paul's in Carinthia has early ninth-century glosses for virtually every word.[1] There is, indeed, a kind of progression from full interlinear glosses of this sort to an attempt on the part of the glossator to make at least some of his German read as continuous prose, and the line between an interlinear gloss of that sort and a translation is sometimes difficult to draw.

Some final points need to be made about the form in which the glosses have survived. The *St. Paul Luke-Glosses* referred to above are typical in that an early manuscript has been glossed in a later hand. Dating becomes problematic, however, when the original and the glosses are recopied. So, too, the usual difficulties imposed by potentially inaccurate copying are intensified. Not only could either the Latin or the German be wrongly transcribed, but the relationship between the two can become confused. Nor need all the glosses in a manuscript have been added at the same time. Indeed, sometimes glosses are added to existing glosses—giving us the concept of superglosses. Sometimes a manuscript will indicate the use of a German word, perhaps by the abbreviations *.f.* for *francice* ("Frankish"), *.t.* for *theodisce* ("German[ic]"), or simply *.i.* for *i*[*d est*] ("that is").

Additional problems arise when the glosses are written in code, although the codes used are fairly simple ones. In one manuscript, for example, the lemma *anus* ("anus") is glossed *brslph*. The code replaces the vowels with the following consonant, so that $b = a$ and $p = o$, giving us *arsloh* (modern German *Arschloch,* "asshole," although entirely literal in Old High German). A later scribe, however, has failed to understand this, and has reglossed the Latin word as *altzwip* ("old woman"), ignoring the context of the Latin and assuming the word to be *anūs,* which does indeed have that meaning.[2] Finally, some glosses are not even written, or at least are not inked, but are scratched on with a stylus. Such *Griffel-Glossen* ("stylus-glosses") only become visible when carbon graphite dust is applied to the manuscript.[3]

Claims have been made for Irish and for Anglo-Saxon influence in the earliest glosses. Georg Baesecke went further, stressing the individual role of Arbeo, bishop of Freising from 764 to 783, as the impulse behind much of the early activity in this field, but such assumptions are of smaller relevance than the question of what the glosses were and what their purpose was.[4]

Various types of Latin material acquire German glosses, and they can be summed up once more in a schematic and not a chronological fashion. Reference has been made already to Latin synonym lists, and indeed, one of the earliest texts with German glosses is a compendium of synonyms, headwords in alphabetical order followed by several words or phrases with the same meaning. The text is known from the opening Latin word as *Abrogans,* and this reminds us that the order of the German words it contains still follows the Latin alphabetization. A second type of Latin work—again a useful one—to be glossed in German is the thematic word-list, in which the words are not alphabetized but arranged in topics. An early example is the so-called *St. Gallen Vocabulary,* based on a Greek-Latin thematic word-list called the *Hermeneumata,* and giving, for example, lists of parts of the body. A small additional example that might be considered under this heading is the list of names of the months and the winds found in a Latin life of Charlemagne, and supposedly compiled by the emperor himself (Lb. III). The development of this type of topical gloss leads ultimately to the encylopedic compilations represented at the end of the Old High German period by the massive *Summarium Heinrici.* Glosses of individual works that are not themselves lists constitute the third type. There are a great many sets of glosses to biblical and secular writings throughout the period. Most books of the Bible are glossed, as are theological and canon-law texts, and then, later on, texts as diverse as herbaria and medical writings. Latin classical writers are relatively infrequently glossed, although this does happen. There are rather more glossed manuscripts of Christian Latin poets such as Prudentius or Arator. The glosses themselves can fulfill a variety of functions—teaching and expounding the Latin texts, explaining grammatical points, facilitating private reading. A glossed manuscript might well be of use to a translator or commentator using the vernacular, too.[5] A work like *Abrogans* might serve as a thesaurus for German, too, although the user would have to start from a Latin concept. The main aim of the glosses, however, is likely to have been to enhance the comprehension of Latin.

The large number of glosses extant makes it expedient to illustrate the system with a single, typical example, before examining some major works. We may take as an illustration the Old High German glosses provided for a Latin poem based on the Acts of the Apostles, written by Arator, a Christian poet of the sixth century. The work was well known throughout the Middle Ages. The German glosses are found in a codex from Trier, now Manuscript 1494 in the municipal library, dating from the tenth century. Seventeen other manuscripts with Arator glosses are known, the earliest from the mid-ninth century. The Trier glosses have, however, recently been edited in a convenient form, and the edition also includes some photographs of the manuscript. It must be emphasized again that a great deal can be learned about the nature of the Old High German glosses from the most cursory glance at one of the glossed manuscripts, and facsimiles are readily available. The Trier Arator codex has 377 glosses, yielding 514 individual words. The entire corpus of Old High German glosses on Arator runs to over a thousand words, and the existence of 130 manuscripts of the Latin poem gives evidence of its general popularity.[6]

The Trier codex (which contains other Latin works, too, some of them glossed) sets the poem itself out as verse, with large capitals for each line, giving two wide margins and plenty of space between lines. The text is in one handwriting, and another hand has added Latin chapter titles. A third hand has added, in both margins, explanatory passages in Latin prose. Between the lines and sometimes in the margins are both Latin and Old High German glosses. Thus above the first word of the Latin phrase *Innocuos mactare greges* ("to slaughter the innocent flocks") has been added the single German word *unscadeliu* ("innocent"—in the accusative plural, like the Latin). That example is a simple gloss. More complicated is a passage that occurs subsequently. Here the Latin line reads "obscurum praevenit opus lectisque maniplis" ("he hindered the secret plan, and, having chosen the soldiers. . ."). Here the first word carries a *Latin* gloss, *intercep*[*it*] with an abbreviated ending, and next to this the German equivalent, *Undernam*. The word *maniplis* is glossed first *militib*[*us*] and then *scaroN* ("troops"). A long Latin comment on *maniplis* fills the right-hand margin.

Space is always a problem, even with a widely set basic text like this one. Near the phrase *Nudus amore timor* ("fear stripped of love") we find in the margin the gloss *Nitedardazdurohsine liubi,* which can be resolved into seven words: *Ni teda* [*e*]*r daz duroh sine liubi* ("he did not do it because of his love"), a gloss which is really an explanatory paraphrase. That gloss could be resolved, but even in a relatively clear text like this one enigmas occur, as a final, somewhat complex example shows. The text is "Praefertur imago / Quattuor ordinibus se submittentibus" ("The picture dips down at four points"). Here *ordinibus* is provided with a Latin synonym and then a German one. But just before these glosses comes the explanatory line "quadrangulum erat illud uas" ("this implement was square"), and just before that, in the left-hand margin, the German words *fierekke ste.* The first element presumably means "square" once more, but *ste* is unclear. At the right-hand end of the line there is a further interlinear gloss, *fierscozzin,* also meaning "square," and the problem of the left-hand gloss cannot be solved by reference to other Arator texts.

Special attention may be paid to one or two individual works of major importance. The *Abrogans* (Ahd. Gl. I, 1–270) is probably the oldest of the glosses, perhaps predating the catechetical translations.[7] The work is, as noted, a thesaurus, of considerable use in a monastery for the composition of Latin, and valuable in its glossed form perhaps most notably as a teaching aid for the understanding of Latin. There are three major manuscripts, a Bavarian text now in Paris, another in St. Gallen—these two are both of the eighth century—and a third from the Reichenau, now in Karlsruhe. The St. Gallen text is probably the oldest, but the Paris codex seems to preserve a more original form: it is laid out with interlinear German glosses. It may have been written at the monastery of Murbach, which was a center of interlinear glossing.

The original thesaurus is one of several comparable Latin texts, some of which were also glossed in German, and indeed, the *Abrogans* itself was revised, perhaps at the end of the eighth or beginning of the ninth century, in a form of which one text and seven fragments survive. This is the *Samanunga* [Collection] (Ahd. Gl. I, 3–270, parallel with *Abrogans*),[8] sometimes known, through a false linking with Hrabanus Maurus of Fulda, as the "Hrabanus Glossary." *Abrogans* itself used to be ascribed to a monk called Kero of St. Gallen, and the name "Kero-Hrabanus Group" is still sometimes encountered.

The original Latin text of the *Abrogans* is unknown. Copying, with adaptation into a context-gloss form, can easily lead to error, and this must be borne in mind when assessing the level of the glossing, which sometimes contains apparent errors.

On example may serve to illustrate the layout of the text as such. In the Paris manuscript, the headword *aegris* ("sick") is followed by three synonyms: *inbicilis* ("weak"), *inualidis* ("infirm"), and *molestis* ("troubled"). These are glossed in German *undaralih*, *uuaih*, *unmahtic,* and then once again *uuaih*—the use of the same German word for two different Latin words, showing a regular problem for the glossator.

The glossator worked from the Latin individual words, and the context, the sense-area linking them in groups, was not always in the forefront of his attention, although sometimes the context *has* been used to establish the meaning. To take an example from Jochen Splett's major commentary on *Abrogans,* the Latin lemma *bucca* ("cheek") is given by the glossator its late Latin meaning, "mouth" (as in modern French *bouche*). In context, the Latin follows this with *gene,* also meaning "cheeks," and supplied in any case with an explanation, *loca super buccas* "upper cheeks." Having taken *bucca* as mouth, however, the glossator interprets the next, and presumably unfamiliar, word with its literal addition "above the *bucca*" as something above the *mouth,* translating it as *grana,* "mustache" (Ahd. Gl. I, 164). At other times, confusion has occurred in spite of the context, and Latin words may be misinterpreted, as when *adulter* ("adulterer") is mistaken for *ad ultimum* ("to the ultimate"). On still further occasions, the Latin text has become confused, and sets of synonyms have been run together, leading to comparable confusion in the glossing. Proper evaluation of the *Abrogans* requires investigation of the whole tradition of Latin glossaries of which it is part.

A slightly later, and in this case thematic, glossary worthy of attention is the *St. Gallen Vocabulary,* more properly known as the *German Hermeneumata* (Ahd. Gl. III, 1–8). The *Hermeneumata* dates back to the third century and was originally used as a topically arranged vocabulary book for the learning of Greek. The German adaptation of it was once again made in all probability at Murbach, although the sole text is a St. Gallen manuscript of about 790.[9]

Much later—in the tenth and eleventh centuries—we reach the fullest development of the gloss tradition in the form of a major, although still relatively little-studied, compendium known as the *Summarium Heinrici,* a work composed perhaps in Lorsch around 1020, although later dates have been suggested. The work has an immensely complex manuscript tradition, with adaptations down to the fourteenth century, when it became a basis for a dictionary in the modern sense. In origin, the encyclopedia seems to have comprised ten thematically arranged books (based on the encyclopedic works of the Latin writer Isidore of Seville and others), plus an alphabetical eleventh book. The many manuscripts vary in format and extent, but those we have tend to be written with German glosses in context (or with spaces left for the German glosses). Some manuscripts have additional marginal or interlinear glossing in Latin or German. The work has a Latin prose prologue, making it clear that the *Summarium* was intended for pupils learning Latin, and the first book deals with Latin grammar: it is unglossed. In addition to the prose prologue there is a metrical introduction in which the beginnings and ends of the lines spell out the title "Heinrici summarium id est" [This Is Henry's Compendium], and it has been supposed that some of the glossing came from the compiler himself, so that already at the beginning we come close to the concept of the dictionary proper. The other books of the compendium deal with rhetoric, men and angels, vegetables, astronomy (with much valuable vocabulary in the field of natural science), gems, the city, people and offices, vestments, and war. To take an example from the fourth book, on vegetables, we are given an etymology of the palm tree and the laurel: "Palma *palmbŏm* quod oppansis sit ramis in modum palme hominis. Laurus *lorbŏm* a verbo laudis quasi laudus" ("Palm, *Palmbaum* because the branches are spread out like a human palm. Laurel, *Lorbeer* from laud, praise . . .").[10]

Between *Abrogans* and the *Summarium* fall many other thematic glosses (Ahd. G1. III), and the range of glossed manuscripts, or of themes with a single manuscript, can be extensive.[11] It is, on the other hand, relatively simple to typify the biblical glosses. Reference has been made already to the *St. Paul Luke-Glosses*. Although the manuscript comes from St. Paul's in Carinthia, it was probably made on the Reichenau. The two surviving leaves have almost every word glossed, under and above the line, and in the margins. The Reichenau, as a major center, produced other relevant glosses, and since these are sometimes found put together in collective manuscripts, they are referred to by initials. *Gloss Rd,* for example, is a Latin-German glossary of biblical words arranged in alphabetical order, originally from the Reichenau and now in Karlsruhe (Ahd. G1. I, 271–95). Such works are either alphabetically based or follow the order in which the Latin words appear in the biblical texts. Most of the books of the Bible are glossed, of course, as were the works of theological writers such as St. Isidore of Seville, or Aldhelm, and the writings of Christian-Latin poets like Arator. There are some Vergil glosses (Ahd. G1. II, 625–726), but classical writers are less commonly treated.

The many glosses—most of them admittedly small—that are still being discovered and edited continue to make clear how important an activity this was, and the number of places at which the work was carried out is larger than was once thought. The major centers remain Fulda in the north, Freising in Bavaria, and St. Gallen, Reichenau, and Murbach in the south. The aim of the work was to elucidate Latin and to teach it to monks. But the implications for the building up of a German vocabulary, even if this was not a primary aim, are considerable.[12]

Phrasebooks

A special position is occupied by two Old High German phrasebooks. The first forms part of the *Kassel Glosses* (Ahd. G1. III, 9–13; Lb. V/1), in the same manuscript as the *Exhortatio ad plebem Christianum,* in a different hand, but also dating from about 800. The *Kassel Glosses* are in the tradition of the *Hermeneumata,* but among the usual brief parts-of-the-body glosses come useful sentences like "skir min fahs" ("give me a haircut") and straight questions such as "sage mir uueo namun habet deser man" ("tell me what that man's name is"), plus exercises in verb-forms. Rather later comes an enigma, however. Following the phrases "sapiens homo *spaher man*" ("clever man") and "stultus *toler*" ("fool") comes a sentence, perhaps as practice, in Latin and in German, to the extent that "Italians are stupid, Bavarians are clever." What the phrase is doing there is hard to imagine. The contrast is proverbial, and is found in later German texts. In a Bavarian text it may just be a humorous exercise. The glossing is quite normal throughout, however—first Latin, then German.

This is not the case with a far more interesting phrasebook, in a manuscript now in Paris (but with one leaf in the Vatican). The manuscript contains a glossary related to *Abrogans,* with some German words, but marginally and on spare leaves is a list of parts of the body, from the *Hermeneumata* tradition, followed by a selection of, in places, highly colloquial phrases, written perhaps in the late ninth or early tenth century. The *Paris Phrasebook* (referred to as the *Pariser* or *Altdeutsche Gespräche,* Ahd. Gl. V, 517–24; Lb. V/2) is unusual in placing the German first, then the Latin. In this case, the Latin seems to provide a meaning for the German, rather than the other way around. The work is not really a gloss, but what looks like a phrasebook for travelers abroad. Where the work was copied is unclear. What is of interest is the collection of phrases, which seem to reflect real or imaginary situations. If the latter, the work demonstrates—in the words of a somewhat overdone paper on the subject—"the hazards of travel in medieval Germany."[13]

The text is difficult because the language shows strong Romance influence: it is Old High German with a French accent. Initial *h* is dropped in German and Latin, and initial *uu* (*w*) appears as *gu-* on many occasions. Endings are swallowed up, and it takes considerable guesswork to interpret *an* as (*h*)*an*(*t*) ("hand") or *esconae chanet* as *sconi kneht* ("good servant"). More surprising still is the content of some of the phrases. While some are useful—"where do you come from?"—some sound a little menacing: "Ghanc hutz" ("go away"). Others are either abusive or obscene: "Vndes ars in tine naso" ("dog's ass up your nose"), "Guanna sarden ger" ("when did you screw?"). An inexplicable alternation in the phrases does make parts of the work look like questions and answers, but there are also paradigmatic lists: "Gimer min ros . . . min schelt . . . min spera" ("Give me my horse, my shield, my spear"). The homely phrase "have a drink, brother" is present, too; but this is found, although by the same scribe, among some fragments of an Old High German Gospel-translation in the Paris manuscript, and the connection is unclear.

The same hand has included some place-names from the area around Sens, in northern France, which may be the original home of the work. A case has been made for an association with Lupus, abbot of Ferrières from 837–862, partly German and trained at Fulda, who is known to have sent monks from Sens or Ferrières to monasteries with which he maintained connections in Germany, possibly to Trier. Perhaps the *Paris Phrasebook* is a language exercise or even a genuine phrasebook. Much remains a matter of speculation, but the text affords an interesting glimpse into a different language register, and the phrases that stay in mind are those of exasperation: "Begott eh ne uitst nen hurt" ("By God, I can't understand a word!").

Interlinear Texts

It is tempting to view the complete word-for-word or even syllable-for-syllable glossing of continuous prose or verse as a kind of intermediate stage between isolated word glosses or the glossing of word-lists, and the syntactically accurate translation proper. Chronologically, this is not possible: just as single-word glosses are found throughout Old High German, so too are completely glossed texts, even if the earliest examples appear a little after works like the *Abrogans*. A number of major full interlinear glosses were completed in the period between 800 and 820, however, many of them linked, as were the *St. Paul Luke-Glosses,* with the Reichenau or its sister-monastery at Murbach. Nor, indeed, is it even justified to place the full glosse schematically as a step toward full translation. The complete glossing of a text does not, and does not intend to, achieve a coherent translation of the original, and it is misleading to speak of "interlinear translations"—especially when this leads to a criticism of the result as "slavish imitation." It is also misleading to print—as sometimes happens—these interlinear glosses without the Latin, as if they were independent. They are not. At best, a full interlinear gloss can begin to take account of the context of the Latin, and, intentionally or accidentally, it can look at times like a syntactical translation. It is a curious fact that genuine translations of Latin works are sometimes found written in an interlinear position, but here the words do not, of course, correspond, except by accident. The initial intention of a gloss, however full, and of a translation is not the same.[14]

One of the earliest and most important of the full glosses is an Alemannic interlinear text of the *Rule of St. Benedict* (St. XXXVI). The work expresses in seventy-three chapters how the monks of the Benedictine order—the sole order in Germany in our period—were to live, work, and pray, and it stresses their vows of poverty, chastity, and obedience. Charlemagne ordered the observance of the Rule in monasteries throughout the empire, and its importance is self-evident. The surviving German text is in a manuscript from St. Gallen, although the original was probably composed at the Reichenau.[15] Other versions must have existed, and there are Latin manuscripts with isolated word-glosses (Ahd. G1. II, 49–54). The St. Gallen text is the work of several scribes and contains (as do the *St. Paul Luke-Glosses* and other texts to be considered in this context) abbreviations that consist sometimes of a final syllable only, as when *propheta* ("prophet") is glossed *go* for *uuizzago*. There are also double glosses, and on one occasion a quadruple gloss, the synonyms depending in fact upon the *Samanunga,* the later version of *Abrogans.* As the text continues, the glossing becomes incomplete, develops into isolated word-glosses, and eventually disappears altogether at Chapter 67.

The exact relationship between the German and Latin texts is a problem, since they do not match. The German glosses fit, however, a more usual version of the Rule than that found in the codex. Thus in Chapter 67 (St., p. 272) the Latin word *propter* ("because of") is rendered *ana* ("except"), which glosses *praeter,* the word found in other versions of the Rule. Interestingly, a later hand has corrected the *Latin* at this point. There are, on the other hand, some genuine errors, as when *officina* ("place of office") is rendered *ambaht,* meaning "office," "position," and presumably translating *officia* (St., p. 206), and sometimes adjectives are mistaken for nouns and provided with articles in German. Errors of that sort can easily occur in an interlinear process, however, and they are relatively few in number: the achievement is a major one in its own terms.

The *Benedictine Rule* also shows the adaptation into German of new concepts with some clarity. A detailed linguistic analysis by Werner Betz indicates the preeminence of loan-meaning in the religious words—a new sense applied to an existing word—and the smaller number of pure borrowings.[16] That the loan words have the best survival record into Middle High German, however, is explained on the grounds that there simply are no easily found alternatives.

Psalms and canticles (hymnlike passages in the Old or New Testament) form an important part of monastic life, both as part of the liturgy and as early texts taught to novices. The service of lauds, morning prayers, involved the singing of Psalms and canticles. An interlinear text of the Psalms in Alemannic is known from a damaged and fragmentary manuscript probably written at the Reichenau from a Murbach original early in the ninth century. It contains parts of Psalms 107–8, 113–14, 123–24, and 128–30.[17] Rather later—in the tenth century—come the Rhenish Franconian canticles (St. XXXIX, Lb. XVII/5), again fragmentary, but with five of the Old Testament canticles used in the lauds service. There are, further, interlinear Psalms from the Low German area, and from the border between High and Low German. Psalms 1, 2, and some of 3 survive in a Middle Franconian interlinear text, and Psalm 18 and Psalms 53:7 to 73:9 in Old Low Franconian, although all of these are known now only from late transcripts or printed versions. Dating is very difficult, and for the Low Franconian texts dates as far as four hundred years apart have been suggested.[18] All, however, are stricly interlinear glosses, as distinct from the actual translations of the Psalms made by Notker Labeo in the eleventh century as they are from those made by Luther in the sixteenth.

Two final works require mention, both originating, probably, from the Reichenau. The *Carmen ad Deum* [Song to God] (MSD LXI; St. XXXVII; Lb. XV) is laid out as a context-gloss, German after Latin, but must originally have been interlinear. The poem is brief—about thirty lines— and the glossator again seems to have misunderstood the Latin at times, although the original text is difficult in places. Of far greater significance are the twenty-seven Latin hymns (numbered I–XXVI, plus XXVa), the interlinear texts of which are referred to collectively as the *Murbach Hymns.* The manuscript, now in Oxford, is a composite one, and the hymns fall into two parts. Hymns I to XXI were written by one scribe, and the rest of the hymns, which come first in the manuscript as it is now, were written down by a different man, who also wrote an Old High German glossary. The first hymns were either written at the Reichenau, or transcribed in Murbach from an original from the other monastery. The later hymns were added at Murbach. The style of the glossing points to Reichenau—there are the same abbreviations as those encountered earlier, and there are comparable double glosses.[19]

The Latin hymns are composed in strophes of four lines, in iambic tetrameter, and were used liturgically. The rubric states that these hymns are "to be sung in the course of the year," and the liturgical position of each of them can be determined, although it is indicated only for the first. There has been much speculation on the reason for the glossing. One idea is that Murbach, as a monastery near the French border, might have been concerned with teaching German to monks of other backgrounds. The double glosses, then, would have served not only to elucidate the Latin, but to provide German language practice. A monastic record notes that the Reichenau possessed "diverse songs for teaching German," but the Latin word used—*carmina* ("songs")—is that normally applied to non-religious works; the Murbach texts are plainly *hymni* ("religious songs"). In spite of the Reichenau note, the glossing of the Murbach hymns is more likely to have been aimed at a proper understanding of the Latin, especially in view of the religious and liturgical role of the texts.

One interesting feature of the glossing, however, is that the glossator does seem from time to time to have worked in a literary spirit, using vocabulary that is strongly associated with Germanic secular poetry, and—another germanic feature—sometimes making his German "lines" alliterate (although the syntax does not, of course, fit). The vocabulary is in general varied, not only in the double glosses but in different occurrences of the same word—*conditor* ("maker") has five synonyms. All in all, the Murbach hymns seem to be interlinear glosses with at least a potential for development. The end result is still a gloss, however, and the separate printing of the German words, even if they look metrical, is not really justified. Interlinear glossing is a separate technique which continues in use as a teaching method with some resilience: it was widely used for the teaching of classics well into the nineteenth century.

Faithful Translation

In moving from glosses to texts in which the German words relate to each other syntactically we may deviate from a strict chronology to consider first a German Gospel translation of about 830, and after that a group of writings from the end of the previous century. The justification for this reversal of chronological order is that the Gospel translation—although in a schematic sense only—comes rather closer to the technique of the glosses than the eighth-century pieces. The reversal of order in the placing of these works does not, however, imply any judgment about the relative merits of the works concerned as translations. Modern ideas of what constitutes a "good" translation (and some of those ideas were voiced by King Aelfred the Great in the ninth century, and have continued to be voiced at intervals ever since) might well cause the reader to respond to the texts in question in different ways. The translations are indeed different from one another, but there may well be quite deliberate reasons behind this difference.

The Old High German Tatian translation[20]—the largest body of German prose before the end of the tenth century, and so of some importance linguistically—seems at first to present fewer problems than some of the texts encountered so far. In a manuscript that has been in St. Gallen since at least the thirteenth century, we have in beautifully written parallel columns a Latin and a German text of the Gospel harmony composed by Tatian. The German was written by six different scribes (some of whom wrote more than one section) and these are distinguished by the first letters of the Greek alphabet, *alpha* through *zeta*. Scribe *zeta* also corrected the whole text. Comparison of the German and the Latin might then seem simple. In this case, however, the problems extend beyond Old High German, and some information about the original text and its writer has to be taken into account.

Tatian was a Syrian Christian flourishing in the later part of the second century. He composed a *Diatessaron* ("Put together from four"), a life of Christ from the four Gospels. His text was used in the Syrian church for some centuries after his death. The language in which he composed may have been Syriac, but was more probably Greek, and Latin versions of his Gospel-harmony were made at an early stage. We possess no original text, however, so that all our judgments on its form must be made from surviving versions in other languages, not only Latin but Armenian, Arabic, or Persian. One major point of interest for the Western, Latin tradition, however, is that the Latin *Diatessaron* predates the Vulgate version of the Bible, the standard Latin text produced in the fourth century by St. Jerome to counter the variety of texts of the Gospels then circulating. The Vulgate was itself revised over the centuries, but the *Diatessaron* in its Latin form preserved pre-Vulgate Gospel readings.

A Latin *Diatessaron* long thought to be the basis for all other Western versions belonged to the monastery at Fulda, and is known as the Codex Fuldensis. It was made in the sixth century by Victor, bishop of Capua, and was brought from Italy possibly by St. Boniface himself. What sort of text Victor of Capua had as *his* original is not clear. The Codex Fuldensis version has, however, been adapted to come closer to the Vulgate, while many of the other Western versions known seem to preserve rather more divergences from the Vulgate. Victor's text is no longer placed at the head of the Western tradition. The *Diatessaron* was, however, popular throughout the Middle Ages, as might be expected of a convenient summary of the Gospels, and versions are known as well in Dutch, Italian, and Middle English. A major Old Saxon poem, the *Heliand* (discussed in Chapter 7) is, moreover, based on the harmony.

Much work has been done in recent years in grouping the various translations and assessing their value as evidence for the "original" text. A major problem in the use of vernacular versions is the extent to which, unless a divergence from other texts or from the Vulgate is very obvious, the demands of the vernacular language itself have been taken into account. In the case of the Old High German text, for example, an apparent deviation from known Latin versions of the *Diatessaron* might be explained in various ways: it might represent a pre-Vulgate form; or it may show the influence of a different source entirely—Johannes Rathofer has pointed to links between our text and other Gospel manuscripts in Fulda; or it may, with a small deviation, be simply that the translator is operating with slightly more freedom than in other places. The vernacular versions of the *Diatessaron* need to be evaluated with some caution both by theologians and by students of the developing German language. Peter Ganz has commented that we are still at the beginning of Tatian scholarship, and Rathofer has properly called for a new edition of the German text. This somewhat pessimistic picture must serve to indicate the extent of the unresolved problems that surround the work.[21]

Returning to the St. Gallen manuscript, the position here is less simple than it might seem. Although once assumed to be the original of the translation, this text seems more likely to be a copy, made in about 840–850. The translation was not made in St. Gallen: the language is predominantly East Franconian, and the presence of Victor's manuscript in Fulda has led to the locating of the origins of the German text in that monastery, although other East Franconian centers, such as Würzburg or Bamberg, are possible. Confident assertions that scribe *alpha* was Hrabanus Maurus, and *gamma* (who has Alemannic features) his pupil and later abbot of St. Gallen, Walahfrid Strabo, have also been abandoned. Moreover, the Latin text does not match the German in the next column or Victor's text exactly—the situation recalls that with the interlinear *Benedictine Rule*. We know, finally, that other manuscripts of the German *Diatessaron* existed—four or five at least. The Palatine Library in Heidelberg had one, which was taken to Rome and then lost, and there was one in Langres. The brief extracts in the *Paris Phrasebook* manuscript indicate another text, and a seventeenth-century copy of what was thought to be the St. Gallen version, but which is now claimed as an independent witness to the tradition, is in Oxford.

The German text of the Gospel-harmony would have been of great value in teaching. That the text is scriptural, though, may have had a considerable influence on the nature of the translation. In fact, much of the work follows the Latin (and the divergences and variations are frequently very small, so that we can for general study refer to the St. Gallen Latin text) in what looks at times like an interlinear gloss. Of course, the text is not a gloss, and this is apparent in its layout, in columns. But the closeness to the Latin is such that the work has been dismissed as wooden and lacking in German-ness.

Such an approach to a translation of part of the Bible is conditioned by the knowledge of Luther's achievements and aims—to put the Bible into ordinary German. The Gospels were Holy Writ, and Latin was a sacred language, however, and the translator may well have felt that an ordinary German was precisely *not* appropriate. The very word order of Latin had, somehow, a significance, and although it could not be followed all the time, it is quite possible that a conscious effort was being made to keep the German close to the original. The notion of the *fidus interpres,* the "faithful translator" in a double sense, has been criticized to some extent, but its effect is probably visible here, as in some of the early translations of prayers and catechetical pieces.

The closeness of the German to the Latin may be shown in a few examples, although it must be added that other parts of the translation show what we might think of as greater freedom. More than one translator seems to have been employed in the work, and quasi-interlinear passages sometimes alternate fairly sharply with those in which the German is nearer to what might be imagined to be an accurate reflection of the spoken language. It must be remembered, of course, that it is very difficult indeed to determine with accuracy what constituted "good" Old High German.

Strikingly close to the Latin, and very frequent in the work, are passages in which Latin idioms, such as participial constructions or accusative-and-infinitive combinations or postpositive adjectival constructions, are imitated exactly, although they are not found elsewhere in Old High German in parallel contexts:

Similiter et Herodes uolens eum occidere metuebat, sciens eum uirum iustum et sanctum (LXXIX, 3).

Sama Herodes uuollenti inan arslahan, forhta imo uuizzenti inan rehtan man inti heilagan.

(And Herod too, wishing to kill him, was afraid, knowing him a just and holy man. . . . [See Mark 6:19–20])

The present-participial forms *uuizzenti* and *uuollenti* are noticeable, as is the final accusative construction. The absence of articles in German is a regular feature, although again it is not universal in the text. Indeed, some better-known passages of the Gospels may have attracted a more "literal" translation—precisely without articles—simply because of their familiarity, much as the order of the words *pater noster* is maintained long after changes with other adjectives plus nouns. John 1 begins:

In principio erat uerbum et uerbum erat apud deum et deus erat uerbum. (I, 1)

In anaginne uuas uuort inti thaz uuort uuas mit gote inti got selbo uuas thaz uuort. . . .

(In [the] beginning was [the] word and the word was with God and God *himself* was the word. . . . [See John 1:1])

The omission of the article is inconsistent, and the addition of "himself" seems to be a deliberate effort to make the text more comprehensible. Other passages, too, translate participial phrases in what looks like a more colloquial fashion:

Respondens autem Ihesus dixit: o generatio infidelis et peruersa. . . . (XCII, 3)

Tho antuurtita der heilant inti quad: vvuolaga ungitriuui cunni inti abuh. . . .

(Then answered the savior and said: alas faithless generation and perverse. . . . [The English Douai version retains the participial construction; Luke 9:41])

As far as individual words are concerned, the text offers a range both in techniques and in actual translations. Sometimes loan-words or loan-translations are employed which may well have been barely comprehensible without reference to the Latin. Thus *tunica* ("tunic") may be rendered *tunihha,* which would probably cause no difficulty, although *couti* ("to share customs") in the discussion in John 4 between Christ and the woman of Samaria is translated piecemeal as *ebanbruchen* (perhaps "co-use" might be an equivalent), giving the translation "ni ebanbruchent Iudei Samaritanis" (LXXXVII, 87) for "the Jews do not communicate with the Samaritans" in John 4:9. The word as such and the two names in Latin syntactical juxtaposition must surely have been confusing. On the other hand, words are varied in context. Summarizing the translation techniques of the Old High German *Diatessaron* is difficult, but in general the tendency is toward the word order and construction of the Latin.

For all that, the size and scope of the text make the work a significant one, a first step in a long history of scriptural translation, in which the distinction between ordinary and spiritually faithful German remains significant until Luther's time. There are many questions still to be answered about the text, one of them being that of its precise function. In spite of much speculation in secondary studies, some of the questions of source and tradition may never be answered at all.[22]

Translations

St. Isidore of Seville (ca. 560–636) wrote his tract *De fide Catholica ex Veteri et Novo Testamento contra Iudaeos* [On the Catholic Faith, Based on the Old and New Testament, Against the Jews] in defense of orthodox Christianity and the Trinity against the explicit monotheism of the Jews and later the Moslems in Spain. As the title of the tract (in two books) indicates, it is based on the Bible, and cites it often. The Latin text is difficult, and the work was translated into Old High German in a manner quite different from that of the Tatian translation.

The Isidore translation exists in two versions. The major manuscript is in Paris, itself a copy of a presumed original. The Latin and the German texts are in parallel columns, and the beginning of the whole work is missing. The work occupied seventy-nine folios, and the German is present in the first twenty-two, breaking off in mid-sentence. The column intended for the German remains blank until the verso of folio thirty-three, after which the Latin fills both columns. No translation of the second book is known at all. The second version, made probably from the same original, but in a different dialect from that of the Paris codex, is part of a group of fragments of a manuscript from the monastery of Mondsee or Monsee, near Salzburg, which was dissolved in 1787. Most of the fragments are now in Vienna, and contain portions of five different translations: a part of Matthew's Gospel; a sermonlike work called *De vocatione gentium* [On the Calling of the People] (MSD LIX)—the same title as Isidore's second book, although this is not it; a partial sermon by St. Augustine (MSD LX); an unidentified theological fragment; and finally the Isidore text, also a fragment.[23]

There has been little agreement on the place, date, or dialect of origin of the Isidore translation since it was first edited in 1706. The language is plainly archaic (the orthography of the Paris text is clear and logical), and the text dates probably from the last years of the eighth century, but problems of place and dialect overlap. The text has both Rhenish Franconian and Alemannic features (although the latter may represent Romance influence). It was suggested that the translation was made at Murbach, but this is unlikely. Murbach was a favorite monastery of Alcuin, Charlemagne's palace teacher, who had himself written on the Trinity, but whose views are not the same as Isidore's. The text has not been adapted, however. So too, the translation stands in some contrast to the interlinear glosses associated with Murbach at this time. The text has also been taken as Middle Franconian and as "West Franconian," the putative language of the Frankish nobility in France after the general adoption of French; but such theories are difficult to prove or disprove. Origins in a French center—like Tours or Orleans—or a border provenance—say, in Metz— are possible.[24]

Most critics agree on the quality of the translation, although there has been some dissent, and some investigations of the supposed speech rhythms in the work have been idiosyncratic. It is true, however, that the translation compares better with modern notions of translation than does the Tatian version. Once again, though, the nature of the original must be borne in mind.[25]

The translator's aim here was to make a difficult text comprehensible. Certain techniques are immediately apparent: the German is expanded and augmented in various ways. A subject is supplied for Latin verbs lacking one, explanations are inserted, and so are emphases and underlinings. The opening of the third chapter may illustrate some of these features:

Post declaratum Christi divinę natiuitatis mysterium deinde quia idem deus et dominus est exemplis sanctarum scribturarum adhibitis demonstremus.

Aefter dhiu dhazs almahtiga gotes chiruni dhera gotliihhun christes chiburdi chimarit uuard, hear saar after nu mit gareuuem bilidum dhes heilegin chiscribes eu izs archundemes, dhazs ir selbo christ ist chiuuisso got ioh druhtin.

(Now that *almighty God's* mystery of the divine nativity of Christ has been declared, now *straightaway afterwards here* we shall demonstrate, with *full* examples from Holy Writ, that he *himself, Christ,* is *certainly* God and Lord.)

The italicized words represent additions, and it may be noted as another regular feature of the work that the opening Latin construction ("after the declared mystery") is not imitated but translated. The whole work rests upon the setting up of arguments by the *impii* ("unbelievers") and their refutation, and the German translator regularly adds an indication of whether or not it is *dhea unchilaubendun* ("the unbelievers") who are speaking, making the black and white of the argument perfectly clear.

The Isidore text contains a great deal of useful theology with direct biblical support, and could have been used to combat heresies such as that of Adoptianism, which took an unorthodox view of the relationship of the first persons of the Trinity, and was condemned at various synods and councils in the last decade of the eighth century. It is possible that the translation was made with the instruction of priests in mind, as the work could have been used too in general proselytizing.

The Monsee fragments, Bavarian texts from about 810, pose a number of specific problems. The Matthew text has occasioned much debate, as the translation is less free than that of the Isidore tract, in explanation of which both the concept of "faithful translation" and insufficient skill have been invoked. Recent studies have accepted that the two translations, of the tract and of the Gospel, are by the same person, but the Monsee Matthew does have *some* similarities with the Tatian translation. This may well stem from a desire on the part of the translator to strike a balance between clarity in German and adherence to a sacred text, a middle road which is not the same as that of the Tatian translator, but which comes from a similar impulse.[26]

The content of the Monsee fragments—and the surviving portions are indeed very small—is interesting as a whole. The usefulness of the Matthew Gospel speaks for itself, and that of the Isidore tract has been noted. The Augustine sermon deals with Christ's walking upon the water as an illustration of faith, and the tract *De vocatione gentium* makes clear that "you are in truth children of God through firm faith in Christ." The few lines of the unidentified work deal with the virgin birth and the annunciation, the whole forming a Christological collection with a homiletic or proselytizing bias, texts of considerable functional use. The range of the translations seems to indicate, too, that this sort of work was not unique in its own time, and that German was well able to handle difficult theological texts. That there is a long gap before translations like this are found again is of questionable relevance. The three basic methods of aiding the reading of Latin through German—gloss, faithful translation, and free translation—are entirely separate, but all have the same function, and if a word-gloss serves the purpose, then what need is there of a translation? What must be avoided, too, is the unqualified evaluation of the different types as "good" or "bad" in terms of Old High German. All three types depend on their Latin originals, and simply represent different ways of making those originals clear. Their collective importance is that they show to us the development of a philosophical vocabulary and the ability of the early German language to cope with complex thoughts in a continuous and coherent manner. They show us the potential of the language. What inspired the translator of the Isidore tract to take such clear pains with his language (or why the translation breaks off) we do not know, nor is it clear if, say, the Murbach hymn-glosses actually were used to develop skills in German, rather than in the understanding of Latin. It is more likely, however, that the desire to make Latin texts accessible is far and away the major consideration behind all three types of translation, and it remains so for a long time.

Chapter Four
Magic and Medicine

The most strictly functional of the writings in Old High German are so in a physical, rather than a legal or theological, sense, and are concerned with the curing or prevention of misfortune, primarily illnesses in men and their animals. A number of these writings take the form of charms or magic formulas which may be accompanied by ritual action, but which depend on the power of the words for their effect. Closely related to these are the few surviving Old High German recipes, pharmaceutical prescriptions against illnesses. To these may be added a third category, that of the blessing, formulas designed to ward off, rather than to cure, specific misfortunes. They are related to the charms in a formal sense, whereas the recipes match the charms in a functional sense.

The surviving charms—the largest of the three categories—constitute a history of Old High German writings *in parvo*. They include pagan invocations as well as Christian pieces that look much like prayers. They appear to span the whole era in which Old High German is written, going well beyond it. They are known in prose and verse, and in the latter they survive both in the earlier Germanic alliterative form and in the later rhymed verse. They command considerable interest by providing an insight into a world bounded neither by Christian doctrines nor by a warrior ethos. The charms, recipes, and blessings are all potentially useful to all men.

Medical knowledge and practice in the Old High German period may be summed up fairly briefly. The relatively advanced fund of Graeco-Roman medical knowledge had been lost, or rather, had passed to India and the Arab world, whence it was to return to Europe in the twelfth and thirteenth centuries. Some relics may have remained, but for the most part medical practice was limited to herbal pharmacy and the accompanying use of magic. The monasteries did, of course, have some medical expertise. Monte Cassino, in Italy, was a center, and so was St. Gallen. A ninth-century plan of St. Gallen shows us a surgery (*domus medicorum*) and the

45

doctor's house (*mansio medici ipsius*) as well as an ordered herb-garden. The
Reichenau had an herb-garden as well. To what extent the monks served
the community in medicine is unclear, however. Successive church councils from the ninth to the thirteenth century spoke against the practice of
medicine, either for profit or at all, and medicine passed increasingly into
lay hands, although prayers for cures will have continued. In the Germanic
languages, however, genuine medical writings are rare. Only Anglo-Saxon
has detailed medical manuals of any antiquity, a number of texts known as
leech-books, detailing various cures. German has very little, although a
number of charms are extant. These too are medical, useful (and sometimes prescribed specifically) for the poor, who may have been unable to
afford pharmaceutical ingredients. Their close proximity to recipes is
attested in later manuscripts of medical matters. We may finally note the
beliefs in the origins of disease, either as caused by flying worms—
invisible carriers comparable perhaps to bacteria, or, on the other hand,
diabolical possession, notably in the frightening manifestations of diseases
like epilepsy.[1]

Earlier criticisms of Old High German tended to refer to those invocations with pagan content as charms, to the Christian ones as blessings, and
to treat the recipes under a different head altogether. It is necessary,
however, to illustrate by examples what is meant by each of the three
categories.[2]

The recipe is entirely practical, containing ingredients and instructions
for the alleviation of an existing ailment. It is palliative and not prophylactic. A twelfth-century collection of medical notes known as the *Innsbruck
Pharmacopoeia* has under the rubric "Against the flow of blood from the
nose" the recipe: "burn egg-shell and inhale it via a hollow reed into the
nose." A recipe is akin to a cookery recipe, and indeed, the two are
sometimes found side by side in later medieval manuscripts.

The recipe cited is the second item under the heading of nosebleeds.
The first is a charm, designed to have the same effect, to cure a condition
when it arises, not with ingredients but by magic. In this case the
invocation is Christian: "Against the flow of blood from the nose, say the
following—'The tall Longinus pierced Christ's side and at once blood
flowed from his side. In his name may this blood stop." We may remind
ourselves that the practical remedy followed at once. It may be noted in
passing, too, that while this version of the Longinus charm—they are very
frequent—refers clearly to the crucifixion, others refer to an apocryphal
incident in Christ's youth. It is worth citing the original of the two texts
given, as this will illustrate further problems:

CONTRA Fluxum sanguinis. de naribus. Dicat sic. Der lange longinus trans-
fixit xpi latus. statimque fluxit sanguis de latere. in ipsius nomine stet sanguis
iste.
Iterum. Deserruit reiten eines scala scol man ze puluere prennen. et sufflare cum
arundine in nares multum ualet.[3]

The mixture of German and Latin, although this is a late text, is typical. In
the recipe, the first words are clearly corrupt—*eines scala* must be *eies scala*
("eggshell"), and the first two words are almost impossible to interpret. It
is worth noting briefly the form in which most charms are preserved in the
manuscripts. Typically a Latin superscript will say what the charm is for,
and may prescribe prayers in Latin at the beginning and at the end. Any
instructions for actions are likely to be in Latin, and gaps may be left in the
text for the insertion of names or descriptions. The whole passage may
have a final comment such as *daz dir ze buoze* ("that for your healing"), or
the recipes may assert—as in the above example—*multum ualet* ("very
efficacious"). The dating of German texts is always very difficult, partly
because similar charms recur over the centuries, but also because a manuscript may contain a far earlier charm, possibly updated linguistically. The
age of the charm would perhaps have given it extra power.

For the charms themselves, internal difficulties of classification arise.
There are some pagan texts, but these have all been written down in
Christian times, for reasons that are difficult to determine. Sometimes it is
unclear, too, whether a charm is in prose or verse. What is certain,
however, is that the use of charms is of considerable antiquity. The
Egyptians used them, but some interesting examples were recorded in the
Hindu Vedas—the Vedic period ending well before Christianity. Indian
charms conjure diseases "from the bones and from the marrow and from
the sinews and from the veins . . ." and command a cough to fly away "as
the well-sharpened arrow flies away swiftly." A healing charm calls for
"marrow to be linked with marrow, skin with skin."[4] All these have
German equivalents, and give us a geographical and chronological span of
existence that is of some size. Equally we may refer to a charm in Scots
Gaelic known in the last century in which Christ, curing a horse, "put
marrow to marrow, sinew to sinew, flesh to flesh and blood to blood." The
charm ends with a command for a comparable homeopathic healing.[5]

Blessings are not curative but prophylactic. They may be illustrated
with a blessing for dogs (to which reference will be made again) from a
Viennese manuscript. It invokes Christ and St. Martin to ensure that the
dogs in question are protected against wolves and brought safely home. It

is interesting that this Christian text may actually have been adapted from
a pagan original, with Wodan instead of Christ. There is a certain
closeness to the prayer, but these are not really prayers, for prayer is a
generalized request to a deity, usually referring to the human ethical
situation as a whole—"forgive us our misdeeds." The formulaic blessing is
specific. As already indicated, however, prayers are used in conjunction
with charms and blessings. A later pharmacopoeia, this time from Zurich,
adds several charms to a number of herbal recipes. One in Latin is against
mala malanna, probably a kind of swelling, and commands that the
swelling disappear: "I conjure you, swelling, in the name of the Father and
the Son and the Holy Ghost that you do not grow, but disappear. . . ." To
this command—it is not a request—is added the comment, "say three
Paternosters and then one more." Liturgical prayers are added to the
charm, even though they are distinct from it.[6]
    It is entirely legitimate to ask whether these things worked. Blessings
may always be felt to have been effective, of course, and the recipes may
well have been useful on some occasions. A psychosomatic faith in the
efficacy of the charms may have led to healing, but the fact that so many
charms survive seems to indicate some measure of effectiveness. One
reason that they presumably often *did* work is that they are concerned
largely with transient and symptomatic conditions, be they traumatic (as
with bleeding) or inherited (as with epilepsy). Bleeding will in most cases
stop (particularly if other measures are also employed) and epileptic fits
pass. It is dangerous to speak of "medieval superstition" in this context.
These measures represent what medical help was available. Precisely how
and by whom the charms would be used remains conjectural. Some were
perhaps for private *ad hoc* use—especially those for bleeding—and for the
rest, the use might have been in the hands of individuals with special
powers: rural areas boasted their "cunning men and women" into relatively recent times. More specific judgments are difficult, but the monastic role in copying and preserving charms, blessings, and recipes alike
indicates some ecclesiastical support at least, however much the official
church may have frowned upon it.

Recipes

Only two recipes survive from the early period of Old High German,
the *Basle Recipes* (MSD LXII, St. VII), named for their present whereab-
outs, although the manuscript is probably from Fulda. Three recipes
appear, in three different hands, dating from the eighth century, but the

first is in Latin. The second is a German version of it, and the third a different piece. The texts are all enigmatic, and it is not even clear what the recipes are for. The first two describe an herbal mixture to be brewed and given to the patient "when necessary"—he is also to be fed no fresh food or drink, and is to be attended constantly. This stress on the patient is, incidentally, unusual in comparison with the Anglo-Saxon materials. Fever is probably the illness at issue, and the phrase *danne in iz fahe* ("when it seizes him") recurs, although the text has no further details. The mixture is largely of inert substances and roots, notably plantain (isphagula), a common ingredient, which acted as a kind of roughage. The medicine would have been harmless, and perhaps even beneficial, although in a general sense. The third recipe—the second in German—has the heading *uuidhar cancur,* which may refer to a tumor or lesion. The text is problematic because the scribe, perhaps an Anglo-Saxon, seems not to have understood the text. The recipe calls for soap (or possibly cloth) and salt to be burned with oyster-shell, and for a poultice to be made and applied to a wound that has been rubbed until it bleeds. Eventually the wound is to be dressed with egg-white and honey. The burning would leave a residue containing caustic soda and quicklime, which might burn out a cancerous growth, the salt drawing the ulcer and cleaning it. In certain circumstances such a treatment might even cure the patient. The use of honey is of some antiquity in wound-dressing, and is of considerable value.[7] The place of these recipes, added to a theological manuscript, cannot be explained, however.

Although these few survivals do not compare with the Anglo-Saxon leech-books, the latter are comparable in their turn with the slightly later compilations from Innsbruck and Zurich referred to already. The Innsbruck text has remedies for pains in the head, eyes, and teeth, for bleeding, respiratory problems, and snakebite, as well as for jaundice and epilepsy, in German and Latin. The admixture of charms and prayers has also been noted.

Charms

Although the charms may be divided in several ways, a distinction between pagan and Christian works, and between alliterative or rhymed and prose texts, is less striking than that between the charms that consist of a simple command that something is to happen and those that contain the command element but base it on situational analogy.[8] The two types may be illustrated in the very earliest charms, all probably pagan, although all written in Christian times, and some with Christian overlay. The so-called worm-charms command the disease-bearing elements out of the body, and two charms from Merseburg in North Germany describe how a situation was once dealt with magically, and go on to command that a present situation resolve itself the same way.

An Indian parallel to the worm charms has been cited already. In German, two versions of this basic conjuration exist, one in High and one in Low German, in alliterative verse. The worm, as disease-bearer, is conjured out of the marrow into the bone, and eventually from the body:

<pre>
        Gang uz, nesso,   mit niun nessichilinon,
    uz fonna marge in deo adra   vonna den adrun in daz fleisk,
    fonna demu fleiske in daz fel fone demo velle in diz tulli. . . .
</pre>

(Leave, worm, with nine little worms, from the marrow to the vein, from the vein to the flesh, from the flesh to the skin, from the skin to this arrow. . . .)

The charm has the heading *pro nessia* ("against worms") and adds a concluding *ter paternoster* ("three Paternosters"), but there is nothing else Christian about it (MSD IV/5b; St LXVIIb; Lb. XXXI/4: a Low German text precedes all of these). The arrow mentioned would perhaps be fired away, as in the Indian charm. Although the Low German equivalent confirms the reading "arrow," it has been suggested that *tulli* means "hoof" and that the whole is a horse-healing charm.[9] At all events, the pattern of conjuration mirrors earlier *and* later charms, and we may note also the three-line structure, with an incantatory build-up in the repeated phrases *uz vonna*. A number of later charms exist to remove worms—causes of disease: the translation is unfortunate—from men (St. LXVI/4, MSD vol. II, 302–5) and from beasts (St. LXVI/3; MSD ibid.). One of those for use with men notes that if it is used on animals the practitioner will lose his skill with men. The note is in Latin. The charm against worms in cattle, which precedes this in a manuscript now in Paris, invokes the aid of the sun, but in the name of St. Germain: "I conjure you, sun, by St. Germain, that you cease to shine until the worms flee from this—*dic colorem* ["state color"]—horse" (St. LXVI/3).

The *Merseburg Charms* (MSD IV/1–2; St. LXII/1–2; Lb. XXXI/1a–b) are of special interest. Both are in alliterative verse, and they have been written into a theological manuscript, although both invoke pagan deities. Whether antiquarian interest, outside pressure, or genuine belief prompted their recording is unknown.[10] The two are quite distinct, and the first is, in fact, very unusual indeed in that it is not medical (or if it is, then only as an allegory). It seems to be designed to help a prisoner escape, and works by analogy. It tells how magic wise women (*idisi*, Valkyries) once sat together: "Some made fetters, some harassed the foe, some loosened the bonds." The charm ends with a command: "Escape the bonds! Flee the foe!" Much of the meaning is unclear: the exact nature of the women and just what is happening in the first part defy clarification. The text is followed in the manuscript by what might be a letter *N*, perhaps for *nomen*, the name of the prisoner to be inserted.

The second charm, while complex, is entirely different, in that it is clearly medical, intended to cure a horse's sprain, one of many later horse-charms. The manuscript text has been used already as an illustration of the difficulties of reading Old High German, and interpretations of the various gods named are legion. Wodan is there, as are Sindgund and Freya. Sunna and Folla may also be present, and the horse who sustains the sprain may be that of Balder or Wodan himself. The opening word *Phol* may or may not be a name.[11]

The first two lines describe how Wodan rides in the woods either alone or with others, at which time a horse sprains its foot. The next three lines tell how the sprain is conjured out by spells pronounced by two or four goddesses, and then by Wodan himself, at which a cure is effected. Whether Wodan's skill is a special one, or whether the combined efforts effect the cure, is unclear. The rest of the charm transfers the cure to the present: again the incantatory effect and the formulas as such are familiar from charms in other languages and from other times:

> sose benrenki,   sose bluotrenki,
>   sose lidirenki:
> ben zi bena,   bluot zi bluoda,
> lid zi geliden,   sose gelimida sin!   (6–9)

(Be it bone-wrench or blood-wrench / or limb-wrench, / bone to bone, blood to blood, / limb to limb, let it be as if glued!)

By far the most numerous charms are those against bleeding, and these illustrate the use of apocryphal rather than biblical material in Christian contexts. It may be noted that the distinctions between biblical and apocryphal writings about Christ are less prominent in the centuries before the Reformation, however.

Two legends are of special relevance. In one, Christ commands the river Jordan to stand still at his baptism, and it does so. Sometimes it is John

who commands this. The origin is an apocryphon preserved in Greek, but the charms based on it are very common in Western Europe. The idea, then, is not biblical, although Christ is baptized in the Jordan. There may be a connection with other legends, in which the Jordan stops in order to help Adam pray for mercy after the fall. In versions outside German, it is Mary who stops the river, and in some charms only the river's name is preserved. In all connected charms, however, the flow of blood is commanded to stop as the Jordan did.[12] A charm printed by Steinmeyer (p. 379) typifies many, and contains actions as well. The italicized portions are in Latin in the original: *"For nose-bleeds.* Christ and John went to the Jordan. Christ said, 'stand, Jordan, until John and I have crossed you.' The Jordan stopped. So do you stop, blood of *name him. Say this thrice and each time tie a knot in the man's hair."*

The second story concerns the infancy of Christ; and the various apocryphal infancy gospels contain versions, which themselves are linked with the story of Longinus, the soldier at the crucifixion. In the basic form, Christ and Judas are playing with spears as children, and Judas wounds Christ in the side. Christ heals himself, and that is the event to be transferred to the situation in which the charm is used. The blood which came with water from Christ's side after he was speared by the centurion Longinus, however, is also thought of as having stopped suddenly; and this too becomes part of the charms, sometimes combined with the Judas narrative. A Bamberg manuscript, with other medical material, contains a composite blood charm—these are not uncommon—the language of which is older than the manuscript. The charm begins in prose. "Christ and Judas played with spears. The holy Christ was wounded in the side. He took his thumb and pressed his side and the blood stopped as the water of Jordan did when St. John baptized Christ. That to heal you." The Bamberg charm includes, then, the baptism legend. The passage cited is followed by a rhymed version of the Judas legend, but saying only that Christ was wounded, and a third, prose, passage invokes the crucifixion and the wounds of Christ in the hemostatic process (St. LXIX; Lb. XXXI/6a).

Most extant blood-charms follow these legends, many of them combining elements from the Judas and Jordan stories with the Longinus narrative. One that stands outside the pattern is an Old High German charm (or set of charms) from an eleventh-century manuscript once in Strasbourg but now lost. The text is well-nigh incomprehensible in places (MSD IV/6; St. LXVIII; Lb. XXXI/6). The first part seems at least to refer to the Christ and Judas story, although the names given are Genzan and Jordan. This curious corruption is followed by a single line, which seems to mean "The Lord and Lazakere went over the sand together," although names and incident remain unclear. The final part invokes *Tumbo,* which means "stupid," and is perhaps a mistranslation of a Latin charm dependent upon the word *stupeo* ("I stop").

Other German prose charms include those against swellings and tumors (MSD IV /7 and vol. II, p. 305; St. LXXI and p. 386), diseases of the eye (St. LXXIII), sore throats (St. LXXIV), and what appears to be gout (St. LXXII/1–2). All invoke Christ and the saints. Of particular interest, however, are the charms against epilepsy, of which two early texts survive, incorporating the notion of diabolical possession (MSD vol. II, p. 300–302; St. LXX; Lb. XXXI/8). In its fullest version, the "charm against the falling sickness" requires the practitioner to stand over the epileptic, making a bridge with his legs, and saying three times: "Thunderer, eternal one. The devil's son came onto Adam's bridge and split a stone. Adam's son came and hit the devil's son. Peter sent his brother Paul that he should bind vein to vein. *Pontum patum.* He banished Satan and thus I banish thee, impure spirit, from this Christian's body. . . ." The initial instructions are in Latin, and these continue after the charm to tell the practitioner to touch the earth, say a Paternoster, and touch the patient with his right foot. He should then say—in German—"arise, God commands it."[13]

The situation cannot be explained. There seems to be an allusion to Christ as the new Adam, and the reference to *Doner,* "thunderer," might be pagan, or it may echo the description by Christ of Boanerges in Mark 3:17.

A final group of charms is concerned with animals rather than with people. Many have to do with horses, predictably enough in a horse-using society, and most of these are intended to cure lameness or stiffness, although some of the equine ailments are difficult to interpret.[14] One horse-charm (MSD vol. II, p. 303; St. LXVI/2; Lb. XXXI/7) tells how Christ healed a lame horse so that a man might ride, a situation not unlike that of the Merseburg piece, but with Christ instead of Wodan. Other texts deal with different animals or the land, although these come close to the category of blessing. A later charm against hail, for example, is along the lines of "rain, rain go away."[15] Of interest too is the Lorsch charm for bees (MSD XVI; St. LXXVII; Lb. XXXI/3), which may be designed to ward off, rather than to alleviate, evil. The bees seem, however, to have escaped, and the rhymed charm commands them not to swarm: "Christ, the bees have escaped. Now fly, little beasts / in God's peace home in his

care, home safely. / Sit, sit still bees, St. Mary commands you. / You have
no leave, do not fly to the woods, / or run from me or escape me. / Stay
still. Work God's will." There is a similar Anglo-Saxon charm, addressing
the bees as "victorious warrior-women."[16]

Blessings

Of those texts that are clearly blessings, preventing future misfortunes,
one is similar to the bee-charm. The Vienna dog-blessing noted already
(MSD IV/3; St. LXXVI; Lb. XXXI/2) invokes the saints to ensure that the
dogs are not attacked, but may have alliterated once, and referred to
Wodan. In the human realm, a number of blessings exist for the traveler,
but most are post-Old High German. Only the so-called *Weingartner
Reisesegen* [Weingarten Travel Blessing] (MSD IV/8; LXXVIII) shows age
in the language. It seems to be a gesture of blessing for the parting traveler,
to protect him against possible dangers. The superscript, which names the
Trinity, has six crosses appended, indicating that the speaker would cross
himself or bless the traveler at various points, and the German text, which
is in rhymed verse, begins: "I look as you go. I send after you / with my
five fingers, five and fifty angels, / that God may send you home safe and
sound. / May the door of victory and the door of bliss be open to you, /
may the door of stormy waves and the door of weapons be closed to
you. . . ." The style, the repetitions, and the formulaic diction sould like
a charm, but the work is clearly a blessing. Of somewhat later travel-
blessings (MSD XLVII/3–4), really Middle High German, a well-attested
one with several manuscript versions refers to the journey of Tobias's son
(Tobias 4) and then invokes the saints for protection for the traveler.

One final text, a predictably enigmatic one, comes very close to the
general prayer. The so-called *House-Blessing* from St. Gallen (now in
Zurich, MSD vol. II, 305; St. LXXV; Lb. XXXI/5) guards against a
specific evil: the entry of evil spirits into a house. The blessing, rhymed
verse which has some alliteration, too, has the Latin superscript "To bless a
house against the devil," and was thus perhaps inscribed as a blessing,
rather than used as a prayer. The text reads: "It is good, o devil, that you
know you are a devil, / and do not know, nor can say *chnospinci*." The last
word is unintelligible. It may be a magic word, or even the secret name of
the devil. No etymologies so far adduced have been convincing for the
word.[17] One can but hope that the blessing was effective.

Chapter Five
The *Lay of Hildebrand*

In comparison with other Germanic languages, Old High German has not been fortunate in the extent of its literary survivals. As a result of early Christianization, with the means and ability to write in clerical hands from the beginning, only one poem survives in which the society and ethos of the Germanic warrior is reflected. It survives by chance and in a precarious condition. The sense of loss in the awareness that the work cannot have been unique in its age[1] is moderated only by the fact that the *Hildebrandslied* [Lay of Hildebrand] (MSD II, St. I, Lb. XXVIII) remains a monument of compelling literary interest. That this is so, however, is one of the few things upon which critics have reached agreement.[2]

The text is incomplete. A narrator reports how two champions, Hildebrand and Hadubrand, a father and son, face each other as representatives of two armies. Hildebrand asks about the parentage of his adversary, who tells him that his father's name was Hildebrand. His father had fled with Theoderic from Odoacer, leaving behind a wife and a baby without an inheritance. His father, he goes on, was a great warrior, and must by now be dead. Realizing that his son stands before him, Hildebrand attempts a reconciliation, offering Hadubrand a gold arm-ring. The son is scornful, and tells the older man—whom he takes for a Hun—that it is only by such tricks that he has survived so long. His father, seafarers have told him, is dead.

In the text as we have it, Hildebrand answers that the man who stands before him has never been an exile, that he has good armor and hence a good overlord. These words are probably misplaced, and come better from the son at a later stage. At all events, Hildebrand can go no further. He must accept that after a lifetime of wandering he will kill, or be killed by, his own son. Telling the younger man that he will be easy to defeat and that his armor will be easy to take, the battle begins. It has reached the hand-to-hand stage when the fragment breaks off, in its sixty-eighth line. In view of the economy with which the rest has been told, it is unlikely that much is missing, but there are no indications of the outcome.

The poem is preserved on the first and last sheets of a Latin manuscript, almost certainly from Fulda and now (after a series of international adventures) in Kassel.[3] The language and the orthography of our text contain many problems and more arise as we begin to interpret the work, to consider its origins, to examine its meter and style, to compare it with content- and form-related pieces, to establish the identity of the characters, or, indeed, to guess at why the poem was written down at all.[4]

The work was written down in the second quarter of the ninth century, probably by two scribes who were copying another written version—this is apparent from the scribal errors. Once more, some general questions begin to suggest themselves: what was the copy-text like? Where did it come from? When was the work first written down? Why was it copied onto a theological codex in Fulda in the ninth century? Speculative answers are possible for the first three points, but it is doubtful whether a satisfactory solution will ever be found for the last. We can only assume either an antiquarian (since by the time of writing the style and matter would have been old-fashioned) or an aesthetic interest on the part of the (presumably clerical) scribes.[5] Apart from a couple of throwaway references to God, there is very little about the work which would commend it to a monastic writer.

The language presents special problems. There are Low German elements in the text, and also clear signs of the Bavarian dialect. Occasionally they appear, quite impossibly, in the same word.[6] A mixture of dialects is not, in fact, uncommon, as works originating in one dialect are sometimes copied by scribes with a different dialect, which causes overlay, but the *Hildebrandslied* is extreme. The basic dialect, however, is Bavarian. Line 48 of the text can only alliterate, can only fit, that is, the poetic form of the work, in a High German dialect. Several of the supposed Low German forms, too, turn out on examination to be spurious. Clearly, a Bavarian original has been adapted at some stage into what is intended to be, but is not really, Low German. When and why this happened is again unclear.

In affirming a Bavarian original we have already left the Fulda text. The content takes us further still. The names in the work link with a poetic tradition associated primarily with southern Europe and centering on the figure known in German as Dietrich, who is based ultimately on Theoderic, king of the Ostrogoths (454–526). The area around Fulda has no "local" hero, as it lies between the geographical location of the Dietrich stories and that of the northern hero, Sigurd or Siegfried. Perhaps for this reason the work was taken north from Bavaria.

The form of the names of the leading characters, however, has led to the suggestion that the Bavarian poem was itself the successor of a Lombardic poem, and in 1959 Willy Krogmann published a version in Lombardic. Such an original is in fact quite likely, and Krogmann's reconstruction can make us think about points in the version we have. But the reconstruction of a supposed text in a language which is itself reconstructed needs a lot of special pleading.[7] Given the reference to Theoderic, a Gothic version might also be postulated, and investigation of the saga background seems limitless. A recent study of the themes contains at least one chronology which goes back as far as the Neolithic period.[8]

The two interpretative extremes are a total acceptance of the Fulda text on the one hand, and limitless reconstruction on the other. The former has the stronger claim, but even though the scribes were closer to the *Lay of Hildebrand* than we are, the inconsistencies, repetitions, gaps, and linguistic confusions justify at least a limited amount of textual emendation if we are to interpret the work as a literary monument.[9]

Works comparable in style or content to the *Hildebrandslied* may throw light on the more obscure passages, although such works will be in other languages, or from a later period. The father-son conflict is widely known, with poetic analogues in Persian, Russian, and Irish, and the story of Hildebrand's fight with his son is found in Old Norse and in later German ballads.[10]

The use of two historical names in the poem offers, too, a kind of context. The hero, we are told, had fled with Dietrich from the wrath of Otacher. Theoderic and Odoacer are figures from fifth-century history, although their historical roles were changed in a long literary tradition. In the late fourth and early fifth centuries, the Goths, then settled in the area around the Crimea, divided into two groups. One, later termed Ostrogoths (East Goths), remained in what is now Southwest Russia. The Visigoths (West Goths) migrated to Italy and sacked Rome in 410. Eventually they moved on to Spain, establishing a Visigoth kingdom there; but as far as Italy was concerned, the Roman empire—already divided into an eastern and western part—was at an end. In 476 a Germanic (or Hunnish) leader called in Latin Odoacer (who adopted the name Flavius as a mark of Roman respectability) deposed the last puppet emperor and became ruler of the Western Roman empire. He is styled "king" on his coins, and referred to in contemporary writings as "king of the Goths."

In the east, meanwhile, the Ostrogoths were for a time the uneasy allies of another powerful tribe, the Huns, although they rebelled in 453, on the death of the Hun leader Attila, and defeated the Huns in the following year, the year in which Theoderic, who became ruler of the Ostrogoths in 471, was born. Some of his youth had been spent as the Byzantine court, the capital of the eastern Roman empire; and in the last decades of the fifth century the Byzantine emperor Zeno, conscious perhaps that his capital could fall as Rome had done, proposed that Theoderic retake Italy from Odoacer, a political move that set one dangerous faction against another. Theoderic led the Ostrogoths to Italy, had Odoacer assassinated at Ravenna in 493, and became king, ruling until 526.

Literature transforms these events. In Old Norse and in later medieval German writings Theoderic is viewed as the rightful heir to Italy, his throne having been usurped by Odoacer (in later texts by an earlier Gothic king, Ermanaric). Theoderic is seen as returning from exile at the court of Attila to resume his rightful throne, and this makes him into an acceptable hero. The modification of history presumably stems from Theoderic's long and successful rule after he had disposed of Odoacer. The motif of exile also provides a fictional base for repeated and episodic adventures. A retainer named Hildebrand is associated with Theoderic in many later works, but he cannot be linked with any historical figure.

In its earlier forms the *Hildebrandslied* was probably composed orally on the basis of set formulas, repeated phrases designed to fit a metrical pattern, whatever the context.[11] Some of these set phrases are visible from the poem as we have it, and others become apparent from comparison between the work and heroic poems in other Germanic languages. The opening line, for example, "I heard it said," is a typical formula, and in the poem as such speakers are regularly introduced not only with the same verb, but with a patronymic comment which does not, after the first occasion, convey any new information:

> Hiltibrant gimahalta,   Heribrantes suno   (45)

> (Hildebrand spoke, the son of Heribrand)

That the poet uses set phrases in this way does not, however, imply inferiority in the work. The formulas provide a structure, a formal skeleton upon which the poet can build his tale, concentrating on action and emotion. The style can be visibly skeletal, of course, but in the *Hildebrandslied* this serves to underline the dramatic effects. Sometimes in oral-formulaic heroic poetry a repeated formula can seem irrelevant or inappropriate, but here the repeated patronymics, for example, remind us constantly of the relationship of the warriors, and hence of the tragic irony of the theme.

More extensive comment on the formal or metrical aspects of the work is made difficult by the condition of the text. The basic formal unit is the alliterative long line, surviving more extensively and lasting longer in Old Norse and Old and Anglo-Saxon. The long line is divided into two by a strong caesura, and the halves, each of which has two major stresses, are linked by alliteration—that is, by the identity of initial sounds—in some of those stresses. The most important stress is that on the first beat of the second half-line. With this at least one of the beats in the first half-line must alliterate. Usually the final beat of the whole line does not alliterate. There is considerable freedom in the number of unstressed syllables. Certain combinations of sound may only alliterate with identical combinations (*sp, st, sk*) and vowels with each other. Prefixes are ignored in alliteration. Thus an ideal line would be that cited already: ·

Híltibrant gimáhalta   //   Héribrantes súno

More elaborate codification of the heroic alliterative line may be drawn up, but it is necessarily based on works in other Germanic languages. Equally, there are some lines in the *Hildebrandslied* which do not "work" at all. The importance of the first stress in the second half-line, which carries the alliteration, can be significant in other ways, and the variety which can be achieved through the free use of unstressed syllables is also noteworthy. There is a difference between

bréton mit sinu bílliu   eddo ih imo ti bánin wérdan   (54)

(cut down with his sword, or I myself shall prove his bane)

and the more concise and appropriately harder-hitting

héuwun hármlicco   huittę scilti   (66)

(hewed harmfully the white shields)

One final feature of note is the use of alliterative overlap between the second half of a long line and the next, a kind of enjambement that pulls the poem closer together.[12]

The point of view in the poem is almost completely objective. The nameless narrator professes merely to report what he has heard, and even when setting scenes or describing actions he makes few comments. Most of the work is dialogue: the characters speak for themselves. We are not even told to whose armies the two champions belong, although we are probably justified in taking them to be Theoderic's and Odoacer's. The audience would perhaps have assumed this. The armies play no *active* part, but they are always present, and must be borne in mind. They are an audience, a physical embodiment of the warrior ethos which binds both men and makes them fight, a force of necessity. At the same time they are an implicit sounding board for the reputations of the heroes, witnesses to the event.

There is no suspense for the reader of, or listener to, the poem. The relationship of the men is made clear at the beginning, and the interest lies in the way they realize and then come to terms with the situation. One small point may be derived from the objective narrative, however. Hildebrand, speaking first to his adversary, puts his questions "with few words." He is a man of action, and his preliminary parleying is formal, simply to establish the rank of his opponent. In the first instance of a recurrent irony in the work, the father tells his son that the naming of a single kinsman will suffice to identify the younger man, as he "knows all the people of the kingdom." That Hildebrand addresses the younger man as *chind* ("child") may also be a conscious irony. However well Hildebrand knows the warriors, he does not know this man. Hadubrand, for his part, is only able to name one kinsman, his father. The formulaic use of the patronymic which opens his reply reminds the audience of this before the old man hears it.

Hadubrand's father, he says, was called Hildebrand. He has this information from old, wise men, who are now dead, and this implies already that he associates his father with them, with a generation that has gone. That the informants are dead, however, also makes it impossible to question their words. Their testimony is complete. Hadubrand's other comments about his father are ambiguous. First he tells us that Hildebrand had fled with Theoderic from Odoacer's anger, and adds what appears to be a critical comment, that he lefts a wife and baby "without inheritance" (*arbeo laosa*, 22).[13] If this is critical, however, Hadubrand (revealed by the comment as an only son) seems proud of his father's reputation as a warrior. "He was always at the forefront of battle." Once again, the tragic limitations of human knowledge become apparent. "He was known," says the son, "to all men." But he is *not* "known" to the son, who now assumes that a warrior of such bravery would inevitably have been killed long ago. "I do not think that he is still alive." The irony is complex. The sole lasting monument to a warrior in this society in his reputation. Here the deeds of a hero are being acknowledged, but the man himself is not. The reputation that was desired after death is afforded to Hildebrand by a son who thinks that he is already dead.

Hildebrand does not yet state openly that he is the father of the young man. Perhaps the reference to the lost inheritance has inhibited him, or perhaps it is simply that he is a man used to actions rather than words. He is faced, though, with the very difficult task of proving his own identity, of effecting recognition as a man from behind the function of a warrior. Taken by surprise, he ventures an oblique reference to the fact, telling the son that he has never stood against such a close relative. More important, however, he *acts*. He tries to make peace by offering Hadubrand a gold arm-ring as a gift.

This somewhat clumsy and impetuous action is the true pivot of the tragic action. Hadubrand rejects the gift summarily, and he can hardly be blamed for this. We are told two things about the arm-ring. First, that it is made of imperial—that is, Byzantine—gold, and second that it had been given to Hildebrand "by the king of the Huns." The ornament underlines, in fact, the truth of Hildebrand's battle-prowess—such gifts were the standard form of recognition for valor. But the arm-ring is made of Byzantine gold, probably of coins, and it is recognizable as coming from the Huns, with whom Theoderic is supposed to have been allied in the past during his exile. The young man naturally deduces that the owner *is* a Hun. How can he possibly be any kind of relative? The rewards that Hildebrand has gained for his bravery serve, ironically, to make him look like a trickster or a coward. Recognition of the object has precluded that of the person.

Such gifts, says Hadubrand (introduced ironically with the now-familiar patronymic), must be accepted at spear-point. The "old Hun" wants to trick him and—a further ironical twist—has only managed to live so long by such devices. Hadubrand now intensifies what he expressed earlier as a supposition: Hildebrand *is* dead. This time he cites the evidence of seafarers—once again witnesses who cannot be called—who have told him that his father fell in battle. The deliberate finality of his words summarize his tragic failure to acknowledge his father:

> tot ist Hiltibrant   Heribrantes suno   (44)
> (dead is Hildebrand, Heribrand's son)

With an irony that is intensified still further, this line is followed by the usual dialogue introduction for Hildebrand, Heribrand's son. The words ascribed to him in the manuscript, however, are unlikely to have been his originally. In the version we have, the father comments that he can see by the armor worn by his adversary that he has never been an exile, and has a good overlord. Critics have argued that Hildebrand is justifying to himself the loss of the inheritance, which has seemingly not harmed Hadubrand. This view has rightly been rejected, though, as implying an out-of-character self-pity, and it seems far better to reassign the speech about the armor (lines 46–48) to Hadubrand. There is no complete agreement about the position of the comment, however. [14]

The fact that an unmetrical "said Hildebrand" has been placed in line 49, immediately after this passage, certainly points to scribal confusion. If we accept, too—as we probably must from the rest of the poem—a principle of alternating speeches, then there is much in favor of accepting the suggestion that lines 46–48 should appear only after line 57, and should thus constitute the son's final speech.

Removing these lines makes of Hildebrand's response to the assertion that he is dead a unified and important speech in which he voices with dignity his acceptance of his fate:

> welaga nu, waltant got . . . wewurt skihit   (49)

> (Alas, cruel fate, O God, will take its course)

The line is metrically problematic even after the deletion of the "Hildebrand said." Possibly, too, the reference to God is a later addition (the verse may have alliterated on *Wodan*), and at all events fate, or rather *cruel* fate (*we-wurt*), is the controller of these events. The bid for peace has failed, and with the armies looking on, Hildebrand must fight. His own reputation has been impugned by the son who seemed so proud of it. Hildebrand now states without excessive emotion, the position in which he finds himself. Fate has spared him for thirty years, he says, but now he will kill or be killed by his own child, a word which now recurs. Turning directly to his opponent—there would have been little point in addressing what he has just said to Hadubrant, although the son may have heard it—he now tells him that to defeat and take the armor of an old man should prove an easy task—"if you have any right to do so," another ambiguous line. The son has no right to kill his father, but in another sense he has a right to the armor and trappings when his father is dead: these are his inheritance.

On the one hand the poem is about recognition and identity. On the other it is about the roles played in the warrior society by reputation, and also by material wealth, visible and portable in the gold and armor, and alluded to in the question of inheritance. Wealth of this sort is the physical counterpart of reputation in battle, and the matter becomes very complex in the consideration of the son's rights in the legal and moral senses. What he *has* inherited from his father, of course, is prowess as a warrior. Neither of these men is, after all, typical—both are heroes: the old Hildebrand, survivor of thirty years of battles, and the young man (*chind,* "child"), who has been chosen as the champion of an army, set against his older warrior.

Reference by Hildebrand to the loss of his armor also supports the replacing of lines 46–48 here. Hadubrand, taking up the point, sees from the armor just mentioned that his opponent is not an exile, not Hildebrand, but a loyal Hun. The motif is that of the arm-ring—the recognition of things and not men.

This is the last statement, and nothing more can be done. The older man comments to himself that "the most cowardly of the eastern peoples" could not now refuse to fight. The use of the word *arg* ("cowardly") is interesting. Under Lombardic law the application of this word to a warrior demanded either a heavy fine or satisfaction in battle. This is the final blow, the accusation of cowardice, and it is highly significant that Hildebrand should associate himself even implicitly with the eastern peoples: he might as well actually *be* a Hun.

The stage of the hand-to-hand battle is quickly reached, but the battle itself is not the theme of the poem. Fate is the theme, and the work must be nearly complete. Of the possible outcomes, the death of the son is the most common in parallel versions. A reconciliation is impossible, and a double death would simply be horror. Hildebrand's death would show only the workings of a completely blind fate. Hadubrand would never know.

Interpretations have varied greatly, seeing the poem as political, historical, as a legal paradigm, or as ironic. Above all, though, the work concerns the tragic fallibility of human knowledge, the existential problem of human isolation, and the inability to assert one's individuality in the face of fate and a rigid social code. Hadubrand's tragedy is objective: the failure to recognize or to interpret what he sees. Hildebrand's is subjective: he is aware of his fate.

Yet there is one final paradox. The warrior could not avoid his fate, but one possibility of immortality lay open to him. In the words of a Norse text, the *Havamal* [Sayings of the High One], "Cattle die, kinsmen die. . . . I know one thing that never dies—the dead man's reputation."[15] Hildebrand's line is now at an end. He must kill his only son. But what survives him—has survived him—is a poetic celebration of his most fearful (and in view of his age, perhaps his last) battle. Within the fiction of the saga, the *Hildebrandslied* becomes its own memorial. Hildebrand can have no physical posterity, but his reputation lives on in a work which, despite its isolation among Old High German writings and all its textual problems, remains imposing in its self-containedness, fixed in the society of a Germanic warrior class, but containing problems of identity which sound surprisingly modern.

Chapter Six
Creation and Apocalypse

By coincidence, the only works with a clearly religious content to have survived in Old High German alliterative verse deal, on the one hand, with the creation, and on the other with the end of the world. The works are comparable in several respects. Both have been seen as combining more than one original, and both have been claimed as preserving elements of pre-Christian religion. In both cases, too, the form is problematic. In the one work it is unclear whether we are faced with a poem or a mixture of poetry and prose, and in the other alliterative lines appear side by side with rhymed ones.

The Wessobrunn Prayer

The poem commonly referred to as the *Wessobrunner Gebet* [Wessobrunn Prayer] (MSD I, St. II, Lb. XXIX), and known sometimes as the Wessobrunn Creation, is found in a collective codex, containing several different Latin texts and some German glosses, which came from the Bavarian monastery of Wessobrunn, although it may have been written elsewhere.[1] The clearly written text consists of twenty-one continuous lines of German, with a large initial and some smaller capitals, some division points, and the Latin heading *De poeta*. Printed versions vary a great deal, however. Steinmeyer and Braune saw the work as consisting of nine lines of alliterative verse followed by several lines of prose, but other critics have taken the work as being entirely poetic, even if the line division has varied.[2] With the problem of form is linked that of unity. There are stylistic differences between the generally accepted verse part and the last lines, and some grammatical divergence.

Although there are some features in the manuscript text that seem to point to Anglo-Saxon influence—a star-shaped runic symbol is used for the sound *ga,* and the abbreviation 7 for "and"—the language is predominantly Bavarian.[3] A strong case may be made, too, for taking the work as a poem. It is true that the final section does not fall neatly into alliterative lines, and seems to contain a line which is closer to the rhymed verse associated with Otfrid of Weissenberg. But similar problems were noted for the *Hildebrandslied* and will crop up again with the *Muspilli,* the second work to be examined in this chapter. The "unpoetic" last section does, finally, contain several parallelisms associated with the poetry of the Bible, most notably the Psalms.[4] The work is sufficiently short to be given in full.

> Dat *ga*fregin ih mit firahim   firiuuizzo meista,
> dat ero niuuas   noh ufhimil,
> noh paum   noh pereg niuuas,
> ni nohheinig   noh sunna nis*c*ein,
> noh mano niliuhta   noh der mareo seo.   5
> Do dar niuuiht niuuas   enteo ni uuenteo,
> *enti* do uuas der eino   almahtico cot,
> manno miltisto,   *enti* dar uuarun auh manake mit inan
> cootlihhe geista.   *enti* cot heilac.
> Cot almahtico,   du himil *enti* erda *ga*uuorahtos   10
> *enti* du mannun   so manac coot forg*a*pi,
> forgip mir in dino ganada   rehta galaupa
> *enti* cotan uuilleon,   uuistóm enti spahida *enti* craft
> tiuflon za uuidarstantanne   *enti* arc za piuuisanne
> *enti* dinan uilleon   za *ga*uurchanne.   15

(I learned from wise men the greatest miracle / that there was no earth, nor heaven, / nor any tree, nor mountain, / nor any (star?) nor any sun that shone, / nor moon to give light, nor the mighty sea. / When there was nothing, in no place, / there was the one almighty God, / mildest of men, and with him many good spirits, / and God the holy. Almighty God, creator of heaven and earth, / giver of so much to men, / grant me by your grace true belief / and good will, wisdom, learning and strength / to withstand devils and avoid evil / and to do your will.)

Some linguistic problems remain. The opening word looks like a Low German form, the word for "earth" in line 2 is unusual, and the adjective before "sea" is unclear. In line 4 the word *scein* ("shone") has been emended from *stein,* which means "stone." A word is presumably missing at the beginning of that line, and most editors add a word for "star," although the alliteration then becomes a problem. The abrupt break after "holy" in line 9 has caused editors to assume a gap here, but the manuscript does not indicate one.

As far as the content is concerned, similarities have been noted between this poem and an Old Norse work, the *Voluspá,* a prophetic poem which contains a similar description of primordial chaos. Other parallels have been found with works as remote as the Indian *Rig Veda.*[5] The Christian elements are dominant, however, and the sources are most likely to have been Genesis 1 and Psalm 89. Any "Germanic" elements may be explained by the use—which may have been deliberate—of poetic formulas. The designation "Wessobrunn Prayer" is also justifiable. Although it seems, at first glance, to apply only to the final part, the work moves clearly from an epic description of creation toward a prayer to God as the creator. The work has little in common with the extensive medieval hexaemeral literature, writings explaining and expanding upon the creation story as told in the book of Genesis, and the element of praise is the most important feature.

The divisions provided for us by the scribe with his capitals are of the greatest value. The epic first section presents as a great wonder the chaos before the creation. The second part develops from this: even when there was nothing else, there was always God. The phrase "almighty God" is followed, however, by "mildest of men," and this is perhaps the most vexing problem of the work. Most interpretations take the phrase to be appositional, but it relates more logically to Christ, the second and incarnate person of the Trinity. If the phrase does allude to Christ, then a reference to the Holy Spirit might be expected to follow. In fact the poem goes on to refer to "good spirits," probably meaning the angels, who in some theological writings are created before heaven and earth. One might even consider whether *cot heilac* ("God the holy"), a fairly unusual collocation, might not be a corruption of an original reference to the Holy Spirit.

The last part of the work underlines the Trinitarian idea. God is again addressed, this time in terms reminiscent of the Creed, particularly the Nicene Creed,[6] and the idea of creation is taken up again from the first parts of the work. The words used in this last section frequently echo those used in the earlier parts: *coot, manno, manac.* God is asked to grant true belief and good will—a clear adaptation of the Latin liturgical formula "recta fides et bona voluntas"—and to grant, in addition, wisdom, intelligence, and power. This triad looks very much like a Trinity formula. St. Augustine, for example, refers in this context to *memoria, intelligentia,* and *voluntas* ("memory," "intelligence," "will"). The first two ideas may be mirrored in the German, and the concept of will has been used already in the poem. Power is also found as an attribute of the Trinity, but for the most part in later theological writings. The Trinity is seen, too, as the

creating force. God passes on the triad of attributes when the spirit is
breathed into Adam, and those attributes are necessary for man to be able
to withstand the attacks of the devil and his followers, as well as to do
God's will. The whole theological complex is well known.

The last lines of the Wessobrunn Prayer play on the word "will." Man
needs the gift of good will to be able to carry out the will of God. There is
also a play in the final section with the verb *gauurchan*, which can either
mean "create" or "fulfill." At the beginning of the last section it is used of
God creating the world for man, and this turns at the end into man's desire
to fulfill God's will in that world.

The Wessobrunn Prayer is one of the few texts in Old High German,
and the only one in alliterative verse, that seems to have been preserved
intentionally, rather than as a result of chance survival in a margin or on
spare leaves. The reasons for its preservation, though, can only be guessed
at. The Latin title is not very helpful. It has been translated as "On the
Creator," taking *poeta* as a Latinized form of the Greek word *poietes,* which
can indeed mean "maker"—the corresponding verb is used for the act of
creation in the Nicene Creed. For all that, the primary sense of the Latin
word is still "poet," and a more likely translation of the title is the neutral
"Something Poetic."

Muspilli

The *Muspilli* (MSD III, St. XIV, Lb. XXX) must surely owe some of the
interest that has always been shown in it to the enigmatic word chosen as
its title by its first editor, a word unique in High German but probably
meaning, judging by its context and from linguistic parallels, "the
destruction of the world by fire." The work does contain a vivid description of the apocalypse. For the most part, though, it lives up to Steinmeyer's (repeated) description of it as "the most vexingly difficult of all the
Old High German texts."

As usual, we do not know why the work has survived. The incomplete
poem—the beginning and the end are missing—consists of just over a
hundred lines (precise line counts vary), and it was written in an untidy
hand on the blank areas and margins of a very finely written Latin
manuscript. The manuscript is a copy of a well-known sermon ascribed to
St. Augustine, and it was given by Adalram, bishop of Salzburg, to the
prince who would, in 847, become Lewis the German, king of the eastern
part of the empire. The codex was written, then, during the lifetime of his
father, Lewis the Pious, and the German hand is fairly close to the date of

the main text. The suggestion that only Lewis himself would have dared deface Adalram's gift is both impossible to prove, and unlikely in view of the Bavarian dialect of the poem and the dialect probably used by the king. What is more likely is that the German was written down after Lewis the German's death in 876.[7]

The state of the manuscript presents us, of course, with considerable textual problems,[8] but there are major difficulties with the content, too. The poem opens with a description of what happens to the soul of a man after death. Two armies fight for it, one of angels, the other of devils, and the soul trembles until its fate is decided (1–7). Should Satan win, the soul will suffer, but the angels will bring it, if they are victorious, to the celestial paradise (11–17). Thus every man must do God's will, since he is faced with the prospect of hell, from which divine help may no longer be sought (18–30).

At this point, the theme changes from that of the individual soul to that of the Last Judgment. When the mighty king appears and sets the day, all men will have to account for their lives on earth (31–36). This theme is not, however, developed for the moment. Instead, we hear how the *uueroltrehtuuison* ("men who know the laws of the world") have told how Elijah will fight with, and defeat, Antichrist in an attempt to gain heaven for all right-living men (37–47). But other men believe—and they are described as *gotmanno* ("men of God," perhaps "theologians")—that Elijah will fall, and that his blood will cause the final catastrophe: "when the blood of Elijah falls onto the earth / the mountains will burn, the trees cease to stand / . . . the waters will dry up / . . . / the moon fall, middle-earth be burned / . . . / No man may help his brother in the face of the *muspilli*" (48–57).

The fire will sweep everything away. Where, the poet now asks, is the boundary over which a man has been in dispute with his relatives? The damned, without possibility of penance, will be taken to hell (58–62). Thus, when a man comes before the great judge, it will be better if he has judged wisely on earth. Men are always being observed by the forces of evil, who await a chance to corrupt them. If a man has taken bribes, he is already the prey of the devil (63–72).

Now the poem returns to the Last Judgment itself. The horn will sound, and angels will wake the dead. Nothing can be concealed, and all that will weigh with the judge are the good deeds a man has done on earth. Then the cross will be displayed . . . and at this point the poem breaks off (73–103).

At first sight, there appear to be several conflicting themes. The battle for one soul gives way to a view of the Last Judgment, and there are two outcomes to the battle against Antichrist. This battle description, moreover, seems to be a new beginning in the middle of the poem, following, as it does, what looks like an opening formula, "I heard tell . . ." in line 37. Struck by this new beginning, Georg Baesecke divided the poem as we have it into two. That is, he saw the battle between Elijah and Anti-christ as a separate poem, interpolated into one dealing with the Last Judgment. His view has been accepted by some scholars and rejected by others.[9] In favor of Baesecke's view is, of course, the fact that the theme of the Last Judgment is voiced in lines 30–36 and taken up again at line 63, after the battle. This still leaves open, though, the relationship of the Judgment-Day narrative with the fight for the single soul in the opening lines.

Of greater importance is the question of whether the poem as we have it may stand as a unified work. There is, in fact, a thematic coherence. The battle for the soul between the cosmic forces gives way to the individual combat between the champions Elijah and Antichrist. The ultimate outcome leads first to the *muspilli,* then to the Last Judgment proper. The references to bribes and to boundary disputes are specific examples of human judgments, but they link with the revelation of all sins at the Last Judgment itself.[10]

Two basic strains, a theological and a legal one, are present, and the relationship between divine and human law is seen too in the differing views of the *uueroltrehtuuison* and the *gotmanno* about the outcome of the single combat. If the former are indeed men who understand the ways of the world, then they may well expect the battle to end with the death of Antichrist, an outcome appropriate for a warrior class that would, a century later, summarize the ethos of a battle with the words "Christians are right, pagans are wrong" in the Old French *Song of Roland.* The *gotmanno,* however, are aware that, whatever human expectations may be, divine judgment overrules the temporal, and that the fall of Elijah is necessary to the divine plan.

The poet is, on the other hand, interested in worldly legal issues, and there are legal formulas in the poem.[11] This should not lead, though, to an exaggerated view of the legal significance of the work. The poet may have had in mind the general idea that relatives did swear to the innocence of other family members, but the notion is not in the foreground, and in any case we are told here of the impossibility of helping a relative escape from the *muspilli,* from the fire, rather than from the judgment.

The theological issues are more complex. The two judgments of the soul—one at death, the other in the Last Judgment—are not irreconcilable, however, and both ideas are commonplaces of Christian thought. There are also Christian sources for both versions of the outcome of the celestial battle. The fall of Elijah is the more usual, it is true (see Apocalypse 11:3–12), but the alternative defeat of Antichrist is also known. Reference has to be made in this case to apocryphal writings that have survived in Slavonic languages, however. This does seem to be a somewhat remote parallel, but the way in which apocryphal writings pass from one culture to another is complex. The appearance in western literary texts of motifs found elsewhere only in eastern apocrypha is not unknown.[12]

A model for the concept of the consuming fire, the *muspilli,* has been sought in Norse mythology. Whatever parallels may occur, however, the context here is entirely Christian, and the search for Germanic religious elements is as fruitless here as it was with the Wessobrunn Prayer. The idea is there not only in the final book of the New Testament, but in passages like Matthew 25:31–46; and it must be noted that the description of the end of the world is not unique in Old High German. Otfrid of Weissenburg, whose massive life of Christ in verse is probably contemporary with, or even slightly earlier than, the *Muspilli,* but who must be treated in the light of his formal innovations in a later chapter, refers at the end of his own work (Book V, chapter 19) to the impossibility of purchasing one's freedom from the Last Judgment.

One literary parallel may be noted. The Anglo-Saxon poem known as *Christ III*—it is the final part of a longer work—has been linked with the *Muspilli* on account of some similarities of phrasing, although it is always dangerous to postulate direct links. The English poem does, however, describe how "the greatest of surging fires shall sweep before the Lord over the spacious earth . . . the skies shall be riven . . . the stars, steadfast and shining, shall fall. . . ."[13] The vision of the final destruction is comparably powerful.

The *Muspilli* is a sermon. It echoes the homily in poetic terms, and every idea in the work may be placed firmly in a Christian context. The theme of the homily is judgment, both that carried out by men on earth and that of men after death. The threat of hell, too, is present throughout the work. The earthly legal aspects may, however, provide a clue to the audience of the poem. It sounds very much as if the work were directed toward the noblemen who would be entrusted with the business of law; indeed, the *Muspilli* may link directly with Carolingian reforms in legal practice, with the efforts of the Carolingian rulers to curb high-handed and independent dispensation of justice by that nobility. Legal reform is a constant problem for medieval rulers, and the extent to which a ruling house is able to carry it out serves as a measure of its general efficacy *as* a ruling house. Medieval chroniclers found legal reform noteworthy—the Anglo-Saxon chronicle, a century and a half later, for example, refers to Henry I of England as a legal reformer in the year of his accession, and notes with satisfaction in summary of his reign how he gave laws "to man and beast."[14] A poem could be used as a vehicle for underlining such reforms, and the *Muspilli* may very well have served such a purpose.

The assumption of a noble audience may also explain the form of the work. If, as seems likely, the poem is more or less contemporary with the work of Otfrid, who pioneered the rhymed long-line in a major work, aware of the novelty, and clearly avoiding the alliterative form associated with heroic poetry, then we may suspect a deliberately anachronistic adoption of a style to suit the audience. The form links with the *Hildebrandslied,* and so, indeed, does the theme—a single combat following the description of a larger-scale battle between two full forces. That the choice of the alliterative line was deliberate, but perhaps a little uncomfortable, is indicated by the number of rhymed lines which do not, in fact, have any alliteration. But the heroic tone found elsewhere in the poem (and one of the formulas is, curiously, repeated by Otfrid, presumably as a well-known set phrase) may well be an attempt on the poet's part to speak directly to a specific audience. The work is, at the same time, the product of an age of aesthetic transition, when a traditional alliterative verse-form was in the process of being supplanted by a new style; but the mixture of styles here may not be entirely accidental.

The legal points and the possible support for Carolingian judicial reform offered by the work should not obscure the real point of the work, however. The *Muspilli* is a poem about the end of the world. It presents a clear eschatology, warns the listener throughout of the absolute necessity of right behavior on earth, and if it appeals to one specific group in the comments about proper judgments it does so still in the context of the fate which will be shared by all men.

Chapter Seven
Otfrid of Weissenburg

The most important work of Old High German literature is a rhymed life of Christ completed in the later ninth century by Otfrid, a monk from Weissenburg (now Wissembourg) in Alsace. Three features of Otfrid's *Evangelienbuch* [Gospel-Book] are of signal importance. First, it is over seven thousand lines long, which is far longer than any other Old High German poem. Second, it uses end-rhyme, perhaps for the first time, and certainly for the first time to this extent in German. Finally, it is a deliberate literary product, not a chance survival or simply a piece of functional theology. Several fine manuscripts survive, one corrected in the poet's own hand. Otfrid was aware of the novelty of writing in German, and of using rhyme, and he tells us so in a valuable prefatory letter. His work seems to have had considerable influence in form and content, given the development of the biblical epic in German, on the one hand, and the exclusive adoption of end-rhyme on the other.

Heliand and Genesis

Otfrid was not, however, the first writer of biblical epic poetry in Germany. Two earlier works adapt parts of the Bible into Old Saxon (Old Low German) using the alliterative form. The first is again a life of Christ (which Otfrid may have known) called the *Heliand* [Savior], and the second is based on Genesis. The beginning and the end of the divine plan are thus represented, but very little of the second poem has survived.

The *Heliand* is comparable in length to Otfrid's work—nearly six thousand lines—and four manuscripts survive, two of them nearly complete.[1] The *Heliand* is not based directly on the Bible, but on Tatian's Gospel-harmony, which was itself translated into Old High German. Which text of the *Diatessaron* the Old Saxon poet used is still a matter of debate. A Latin preface to the poem is known from a sixteenth-century copy, but it is not very helpful. We do not know whether the Ludovicus named as the originator of the work is Lewis the Pious or his son Lewis the German; and the home of the poet also remains unclear, although Fulda itself, and the monastery of Werden on the Ruhr, are possibilities. What evidence we have suggests a time of composition between 825 and 850. The poet was a well-read theologian, and he adds explanatory material from a number of sources. Most of his additions derive from the great body of theological commentary on the Bible produced by the Latin Church, and the poet knew the Gospel commentaries of Augustine, Gregory the Great, Bede, and Hrabanus Maurus of Fulda, who completed a Matthew commentary in 820–821. The poet may also have used Gospel manuscripts with Latin glosses, Irish theological material, and perhaps even Anglo-Saxon poetry. There is evidence, too, that he knew such apocryphal texts as the *Gospel of Nicodemus,* a work which contains the story of the harrowing of hell.[2]

The form is Germanic, using the alliterative long line seen in the *Wessobrunn Prayer* and the *Lay of Hildebrand,* as well as employing formulaic phrases associated with heroic poetry. The work may be summed up as a Gospel narrative with theological excursuses, told in a Germanic style. The Germanic elements must not, however, be exaggerated. The form would have been familiar to his audience, and the poet is of course concerned with making his material readily comprehensible, but this is not the same as programmatic Germanization of the biblical narrative. The Germanic elements are a function of the chosen style. As Achim Masser notes, "a disciple of Jesus appears . . . as a brave warrior, a noble retainer, a faithful thane to his lord, for whom expressions of popular kingship and feudal overlordship are used . . . all [of which] is superficial, the use of expressions and formulas traditionally associated with the style."[3]

One passage must suffice to exemplify the work, taken from the thirteenth of the seventy-one sections (or fits). The temptation of Christ in the wilderness follows Matthew 4, and the kinds of formulas in question are clear in the scene-setting:

> Thô hie im selbo giuuêt
> after them dôplisea   drohtin the gôdo,
> an êna uuôstunnea,   uualdandes suno;
> uuas im thar an thero ênôdi   erlo drohtin
> langa huuîla. . . .   (XIII, 1024–29)

(Then he himself went, / after the baptism, the good Lord, / into the wilderness, the son of the mighty one; / he was in that desert, the lord of the earls, / a long time. . . .)

The poet goes on, however, not to tell us about the first temptation of Christ, but about that of Adam and Eve, pointing out that because Satan was successful then, men are doomed to hell. Christ is sent as a redeemer, and Satan, as envious of Christ as he was of Adam, tries to trick Christ the same way. This is not, of course, biblical, but the parallel between the two temptations is developed in commentaries throughout the Middle Ages which see Adam's greed (in taking the fruit) as having been expiated in Christ's refusal to make the stones into bread. The *Heliand* poet does not give us all the details, noting just that Satan "wanted to deceive the mighty one, the son of God, with the same things with which he had tricked Adam in former days," but the making of the parallel at the beginning of the Gospel story betokens familiarity with the theology, and gives the audience the essential point of the Gospel passage as showing Christ the redeemer.[4]

The Old Saxon *Genesis,* found together with the *Heliand* in one of the manuscripts of the latter, has been ascribed to the same poet, but there are probably simply close similarities in style. Only about 300 lines of the *Genesis* survive. In an Anglo-Saxon poem dealing with much of Genesis and known as *Genesis A,* however, there is an interpolation, a long section which was early recognized as an originally independent poem, and given the name *Genesis B.* The interpolated poem proves to be a translation of the Old Saxon work, and in this version a lot more text has been preserved. *Genesis B* tells the story of the fall first of the angels, then of man, in lively style, and with some interesting apocryphal motifs, such as a diabolical council which decides on the temptation in Eden. Eve, too, is presented here as having acted in good faith. The work has much of interest about it, but it is treated largely as part of Anglo-Saxon literature, in which there is, in any case, an early tradition of biblical poetry.

The Background to the *Evangelienbuch*

Otfrid tells us a little about his life in the introductory letter to the Gospel Book. He studied at Fulda under Hrabanus Maurus, who was abbot there until 842. Otfrid was probably there in the 830s, and he is likely to have been born at the beginning of the ninth century, entering the monastery at Weissenburg in about 807 and becoming a monk in 815 or so. In his later years at Weissenburg, Otfrid functioned as librarian and master of the school, and under his leadership the Weissenburg scriptorium expanded, carrying out a large program of copying of theological manuscripts. Various texts, either full texts or glosses, survive in his own hand, and we have copies of his signature. We do not know when he died, but may guess about 870.[5]

The primary manuscript of his major work is now in Vienna, beautifully written, with red initials of various sizes, and corrections in his own hand. A copy, also made at Weissenburg, is in Heidelberg, and parts of a third (known as *codex discissus,* "the cut up codex") are extant. One final codex—there may well have been others—is of special significance. It was made on the orders of Bishop Waldo of Freising (who died in 906), and for the Bavarian monastery the text was adapted into the local dialect, whereas Otfrid's own dialect was South Rhenish Franconian. Otfrid thinks of himself as a Frank, and the existence of a Bavarian version shows a movement away from the home area, a possible spreading of influence.[6]

The *Evangelienbuch* tells in five books the story of the life and passion of Christ. Each book is divided into chapters (28, 24, 26, 37, and 25) of varying lengths. The basic form is the rhymed long line, and these are arranged in couplets. The layout is very clear in the manuscripts. The text as a whole contains 7,104 long lines.[7] The books are devoted to the nativity and baptism (I), to the miracles (II and III), to the passion (IV), and to the resurrection (V). There is, however, some additional material. The whole work opens with a dedicatory poem in the same form addressed to Lewis the German, king of the East Franks from 843 to 876; and immediately before the poem proper begins there is a further dedicatory section, this time to Solomon, bishop of Constance from 839 to 871. At the end of the whole work we find a final dedicatory poem, to Hartmuot and Werinbert, monks of St. Gallen, both of whom became well-known figures. We do not know how Otfrid came to know them, but their work in St. Gallen is likely to have been congenial to Otfrid's efforts as a teacher in Weissenburg.

The three dedicatory sections are marked by complicated numerical patterns and both acrostic and telestich messages: that is, the initial and the final letters of the individual couplets spell out Latin phrases. Latin marginal comments appear throughout, and the separate chapters have Latin headings summarizing the content. One longer piece of Latin forms part of the book, however, and that is the letter referred to already, which is placed between the dedications to Lewis and to Solomon. It is addressed to Liutbert, archbishop of Mainz from 863 to 869, the successor in that office of Hrabanus Maurus, and Otfrid's diocesan superior. Liutbert's date of accession, 863, and that of Solomon's death, 871, provide us with the period during which the work was completed, although it was probably begun much earlier. That Otfrid sent the work to Liutbert for approbation seems to indicate that he may have had a wider audience in mind for it than a monastic one, although the nature of the text, a mixture once again of narrative and theology, bespeaks an audience that could follow sometimes allusive passages of interpretation.

The letter contains several programmatic statements about the work, and justifies the whole undertaking by describing it as an intended counter to what Otfrid calls *cantus obscenus,* which probably means the secular, perhaps heroic, poetry of the laity. Perhaps such works had too wide a circulation even in clerical circles. Otfrid then invokes the example of Christian Latin poets, notes the skills of classical poets such as Ovid, and then goes on to tell us what he has tried to do. "I have put selected Gospel passages into Frankish, and sometimes I have added spiritual and moral interpretations." He has not followed the biblical order, nor did he use a harmony. Rather, he has worked from memory, selecting episodes from the different Gospels. Otfrid apologises for his "poor memory," especially in the middle part. That there are five books, he tells us, is symbolic. The books represent our five impure senses, made clean through the "holy four-square number" of the Gospels.

According to him, German, though, is "uncultivated and barbarian." Otfrid means here that his Frankish vernacular does not correspond to Latin grammatical rules, and he enumerates some differences. So too he finds it difficult—as one used to writing Latin—to get German down onto the parchment. Unlike Latin, German needs the letters *z* and *k,* for example, and number and gender are sometimes unlike Latin. Poetically, Otfrid is aware of the novelty of his form, and tells us that he has used end-rhyme, *homoteleuton* ("same-ending," a term used in Latin rhetoric, where strings of rhymed words could appear in prose). He has also used metaplasm, grammatical rule-bending for poetic reasons, what we might refer to as "poetic license."

The opening part of the first book seems to cover the same ground. It is called "why the author wrote this work in German," but the emphases are different. The German language—here called Frankish—is not criticized, but rather there is an emotional insistence on the fitness of Frankish as a vehicle for the praise of God:

> Wánana sculun Fránkon   éinon thaz biwánkon,
>   ni sie in frénkisgon bigínnen   sie gotes lób singen? (I, 1, 33f.)

(Why should the Franks alone refrain / from singing the praise of God in Frankish?)

Otfrid does refer to the skills of the Greeks and Romans in the making of verse, but goes on, slightly irrelevantly, to point out that the Franks are both as brave and as rich as *they* were. The whole builds up to a climax in which the word "Frankish" is repeated several times to striking effect. The chapter is not, however, simply nationalistic. Otfrid justifies his literary intentions, too, this time in a complex play on the metrical terms of "feet," "measure," "rules"—applying the idea of feet to the desire to walk in God's paths, and linking verse measures with the measures of time allotted to man.

The form of Otfrid's poem is of the greatest importance to Old High German poetry as a whole. His conscious innovation of end-rhyme used on a large scale caused him difficulties, and a modern eye might reject some of the rhymes as impure. Unstressed endings and vocalic assonances have to count as rhyme. Thus *holeta* may rhyme with *ladota,* and even *pád* with *stráza.* Only two lines seem to be quite without rhyme, however. Several candidates present themselves as the possible inspiration for Otfrid's use of rhyme. The most likely is the so-called Ambrosian hymn, a Latin metrical form that both scans and rhymes. In a highly inflected language like Latin, where a series of endings will be identical, rhymes can occur naturally. Ambrosian hymns, then, may have been the source, but it is not clear how and when this type of poetry reached Germany. It is found earlier in England and Ireland, but usually after Otfrid's time in Germany. Perhaps Fulda again served as a bridge.[8] There may, of course, have been a vernacular German tradition of rhyme, and we may recall, finally, the use of *homoteleuton* in prose, even if the rhythmic structure is absent there.

Otfrid's line is, like the alliterative counterpart, divided into two halves by a strong caesura, but the halves are linked by the rhyme. Usually the two halves form a syntactic unit, so that we have a genuine long line rather than an extended couplet. There is some freedom of unstressed syllables, but the lines normally balance. Otfrid's strophe of two long lines, his scansion and rhyme may be seen in the following example, though it should be noted that the manuscripts indicate only some of the stresses, with acute accents. Others have been added here, and the grave accents indicate a slightly weaker stress. The rhyme has to be thought of as carrying at least such a weak stress to be noticed at all:

> Nu fréwen síh es állè   so wér so wóla wóllè
>   joh so wér si hóld in múate   Fránkonò thíotè . . . (I, 1, 123f.)

(Now may all rejoice, who are well-disposed / and who hold dear the Frankish people).

Otfrid's skills as a versifier are rather different from those expected of a modern poet. He makes this clear in his deliberate use of five books to stand against the four Gospels, and also in the dedicatory poems, which have a numerical link (they all have multiples of twelve lines) as well as the complicated acrostics and telestichs. Much recent research has been devoted to the establishing of numerical patterns in Otfrid, uncovering an otherwise unsuspected artifice which is part of his literary intent. His aim is not to express new thoughts, but to express what he sees as divine truth in an aesthetic manner. He is original in undertaking to do so in German, and to use rhyme, and his idea of poetic form takes in a complicated play with the numbers of lines, chapters, and even words, as well as strophic groupings. This implies, of course, two levels of reception for the work as a whole: an aural one, and also a specifically visual response to the manuscript, to appreciate patterns of capitals and strophic blocks. Of course, the search for numerical patterns can be taken too far, and there has been a critical reaction to its overemphasis in the context of some works (and the *Heliand* is a case in point). But Otfrid does give us more to go on, and critics have established in the poem cross-figures, for example, and more involved plays with squared, even, and uneven numbers.[9]

The aural side of the reception is also a matter of debate. In the letter to Liutbert, Otfrid refers to his *centus lectionis* ("song-reading"), which presumably means some sort of declamatory delivery, like operatic recitative. On the question of Otfrid's language, the point he himself makes about poetic license has led to difficulties in distinguishing between that license and what it was possible to say in Old High German. At all events, a poetic work is hardly the best source for questions of syntax and grammar. We may refer, though, to Otfrid's use of variation of phrases for emphasis, and he is quite capable of involved play on individual sounds and words.[10]

Otfrid and the Bible

Otfrid's aesthetic premises are different from those of the *Heliand* poet, and he is not following a harmony. Like the Old Saxon poet, though, he adds explanation and teaching to his telling of the story; and he is, indeed, very much more a narrator and commentator—thus the title of a celebrated critical study of Otfrid.[11] Otfrid derives his additional material from a variety of sources, but in the main the explanatory comments and moral conclusions derive from a tradition of Latin theological commentary on the Bible, stemming largely from the writings of Augustine and Gregory, and easily accessible to the poet in the biblical commentaries of the Carolingian period.

For the Church Fathers and their successors, every idea, event, or even word in the Bible was potentially susceptible of four interpretations, which may be categorized (as they later were) as follows. An historical sense, the *sensus litteralis*, is basic: the event actually happened. This need not imply a literal reading of the Bible in a modern sense. The approach remains interpretative, and the "literal sense" may assume that things happened which the Bible does not mention. An historical interpretation of Genesis 3, for example, explains how the devil speaks through the serpent, even if this is not biblical.

The other three senses of medieval biblical interpretation are all spiritual. The first of these is known as the typological (or allegorical) sense, and looks for the foreshadowing of events linked with the redemption in the Old Testament. It links the two testaments, but in fact the New Testament is always the starting-point. Thus the temptation of Christ in the wilderness was foreshadowed by the temptation of Adam in Paradise. Next comes the tropological (or moral) sense, which draws from the biblical event a lesson for man's behavior on earth. Still with Genesis, the tropological interpretation of the enigmatic comment about Eve crushing the serpent's head (Genesis 3:15) is that sin should be stamped on at the very beginning. The final spiritual sense is the anagogical, looking for references to the last things or to life after death. Thus a comment about Jerusalem might mean not only the place, but also the celestial city, or heaven. This system of biblical commentary—or exegesis—is found in detail in the works of the Fathers. Later commentators, however, do not necessarily contribute new interpretations. A commentary from Otfrid's time is far more likely to repeat the interpretation of a verse of the Bible given by Augustine or Gregory, sometimes acknowledged, but usually not. For this reason it is very difficult to pinpoint Otfrid's exact sources. Commentaries on the major biblical books—the Gospels, Genesis, and Psalms—abound, and we are sometimes forced to refer simply to "exegetical commonplaces." It is reasonable to assume knowledge of the Fulda tradition, however, and Otfrid will have known Hrabanus's Matthew commentary, and the Gospel interpretations of Hrabanus's scholarly forbears, Alcuin and Bede.

On the other hand, Otfrid's additions do not all derive from Latin exegesis. He may have known translations of commentaries by eastern theologians, as well as apocryphal writings, and the liturgy probably influenced parts of his work. It is possible that he drew for his narrative order upon a Gospel manuscript with the liturgical readings marked in. Ideas familiar to Otfrid and his audience may be far less familiar to us, of course, and only recently have comprehensive allegorical handbooks to the *Evangelienbuch* begun to appear.[12]

An Epitome of the *Evangelienbuch*

Otfrid's techniques may be demonstrated by a close look at the way in which he handles a familiar part of the Bible, the arrival of the Wise Men, treated in two chapters (17 and 18) of the first book. Otfrid follows the unique account, in Matthew 2, and adds various incidental points of information, such as the identification of the Magi as astronomers (a point found in Alcuin's commentary). From time to time, he adds brief comments to make the narrative clear. When Herod asks the Wise Men to return to him after seeing the child, Otfrid, first of all, underlines his falsity, and then indicates succinctly the wider implications of this piece of wickedness:

> Lóug ther wénego mán,   er wánkoto thar filu frám;
>   er wólta nan irthuésben   joh uns thia frúma irslegen.   (I, 17, 51f.)

(The wicked man lied. His intent was far from [bringing gifts]. He wanted to destroy [the child] and also ruin our salvation.)

If a point is particularly important, Otfrid does not integrate it in this manner, but breaks off to explain. Later in the same chapter, when the Magi bring gold, incense, and myrrh, Otfrid inserts a subheading, *mystice* ("spiritual significance"). The interpretation extends only over six long-lines, which presupposes a certain amount of background information on the part of the audience. Otfrid here echoes Bede's brief commentary on the gifts, although other commentators are more expansive:

> Ih ságen thir thaz in wára,   si móhtun bringan méra;
>   thiz wás sus gibari   theiz géistlichaz wári.
> Kúndtun sie uns thánne,   so wir firnémen alle,
>   gilóuba in giríhti   in theru wúntarlichun gífti:
> Thaz er úrmari   uns éwarto wari,
>   ouh kúning in gibúrti   joh bi unsih dót wurti.   (I, 17, 67–72)

(I tell you truly that they could have brought more. / It was fitting thus, as it was spiritual. / They tell us, as we all may see, about true belief through the wonderful gifts. The mighty one would be our priest, a king at birth, and would die for us).

In fact, the first four lines do little more than prepare us for the interpretation, which comes in the final couplet. The incense betokens Christ's priesthood, the gold kingship, and the myrrh the crucifixion. The interpretation is actually still used in the English Christmas carol "We Three Kings."

The passage is by no means devoid of poetic power. Just before the insert, Otfrid has told us that the Magi "súahtun sine wára" which probably means "sought Christ's protection." There is a verbal overlap with *wara* ("truth") at the beginning of the *mystice* section, and this then overlaps acoustically with the preterite of the verb "to be." The piling-up of *gi-* formations is also striking and must be deliberate. The sample is small, but similar comments may be made about many indications of Otfrid's lyrical skill, which has never been fully explored.

After the insert, Otfrid tells us briefly that an angel told the magi in a dream to return home by a different path (Matthew 2:12), and this causes him to make a still more positive break in the narrative. He now devotes an entire chapter to an interpretation of the point, this time tropological, although the whole chapter bears the simple heading *Mystice* once more. The forty-six lines open with a general comment which makes clear the theological importance of the excursus. "This journey warns us—we should take heed—that we should seek *our* homeland. Perhaps you don't know what it is? Our homeland is Paradise." The Magi have become symbols of mankind, expelled by the fall of Adam from their country of birth. To return to the homeland—to the heavenly paradise—we must take a different path, that of righteousness. Hrabanus's commentary contains this exegesis, and Otfrid expands it with a rhetorical set-piece on the unimaginable joys of Paradise (which includes a line used also in the *Muspilli,* probably a well-known formula, and one of the two unrhymed lines in the *Evangelienbuch*). He follows this with another rhetorical passage, bemoaning impressively man's state of exile from paradise:

> Wolage élilenti,   hárto bistu hérti,
>   thu bist hárto filu suár,   thaz ságen ih thir in álawar!
> Mit árabeitin wérbent   thie héiminges thárbent;
>   ih haben iz fúntan in mír,   ni fand ih líebes wiht in thír;
> Ni fand in thír ih ander gúat,   suntar rózagaz muat,
>   séragaz herza   joh mánagfalta smérza!   (I, 18, 25–30)

(Alas, our exile! how hard you are, / you are very hard indeed, I tell you truly, / with sufferings struggle those who miss their homeland. / I know in myself that there is no good in you. / I found nothing more in you than tear-filled spirits, / a troubled heart and manifold sufferings.)

Again worthy of note are the sound-echoes (*harto-herti*) and near-repetitions (*fúntan in mir . . . fand in thír*), as well as the sound and metrical balance of *rozagaz, seragaz, managfalta*. The chapter ends on a positive note: those who choose the "other path" and reject the world can reach the homeland of paradise again. Man has been redeemed after Adam's fall.

Christ and the Woman of Samaria

In his second book Otfrid devotes over a hundred lines to the story of Christ and the woman of Samaria (John 4, 3–42). This is absent from the *Heliand* (although it is, of course, in the *Diatessaron*), but another Old High German rhymed version of the story—the prescribed reading for the Friday after the third Sunday in Lent—was written down in the tenth century in the monastery on the Reichenau in Lake Constance. The Alemannic poem *Christus und die Samariterin* (MSD X, St. XVII, Lb. XXXIV) is incomplete and rather different from Otfrid's version.[13] It adheres closely to the Bible, without exegetical additions, and takes the story in thirty-one long lines as far as John 4:20, in which the woman has just acknowledged Christ as a prophet. To reach this point, Otfrid takes almost exactly twice as many lines.

The Alemannic poem tells the story rather sparsely, omitting the frequent "Jesus said" elements of the Gospel text, and presenting us with an epic poem in dialogue form. The point of retelling this particular story is presumably that made in John 4:39–41, that the Samaritan woman and many others came to believe in the revelation of Christ although they were not Jews; but the anonymous poem breaks off before this point is reached. Its plain presentation (in strophes that are sometimes of three, rather than two, long lines) contrasts with that of Otfrid, but his version is part of a larger whole.

Although Otfrid does include the frequent indications of speech found in the original, the effect is not one of excessive long-windedness but of objectivity. Otfrid stresses first the actual humanity of Christ, underlining how tired and thirsty he is at the well, and he explains too why the woman refuses to give him water. He expands Christ's answer, however, with a longer injunction that the woman should listen very carefully, indeed, before reference is made to the living water. The woman still does not understand, of course, and Christ reveals then his prophetic powers.

For the audience, however, the point about the real water (which the human Christ needs) and the living water of the spirit has already been made. The Alemannic poem uses for "well" the words *brunnen* and *puzzi* indiscriminately. Otfrid uses them, too, but has the woman make consistent use of the latter, where Christ always used the former. What is more, he prepares us for this by giving the two words as synonyms at the outset—"*brunnen* that we also call *puzzi.*"[14] The point is Christ's humanity, and the gradual revelation that the man, who is also God, can provide this living water.

Otfrid's Achievement

A full account of Otfrid's poetic skills is impossible in a work of this size, but he is capable not only of narrative but also of sustained hymnic style, for example in the treatment of the opening of John's Gospel, the first chapter of the second book. A vision is given of the uncreated universe, where there is only the preexistent logos:

> Er allen wóroltkreftin   joh éngilo giscéftin,
>   so rúmo ouh so in áhton   mán ni mag gidráhton;
> Er sé ioh hímil wurti,   joh érda ouh so hérti,
>   ouh wíht in thiu gifúarit,   thaz siu éllu thriu rúarit:
> So was io wórt wonanti   er állen zitin wórolti;
>   thaz wír nu sehan óffan,   thaz was thanne úngiscafan.   (II, 1, 1–6)

(Before the world and the angels were made, / longer ago than man can think, / before sea or sky, or the firm earth / or anything that moves in these three, / the word abode always, before all the ages. / All that we see was then unformed.)

The picture of preexistence is built up anaphorically, with repetition of the "before . . ." formula that Otfrid has set up, and then it is underlined with a refrain which recurs five times:

> So was er io mit ímo sar,   mit imo wóraht er iz thar;
>   so wás ses io gidátun,   sie iz allaz sáman rietun   (II, 1, 15f.)

(The word was always with God, and with it he created; / whatever was done, they accomplished it together.)

The opening of this refrain, "So was . . .," has already been sounded, and it is used again outside the refrain.

In other sections, the *Evangelienbuch* compares closely with the *Heliand.* Thus the treatment of the temptation in the desert also invokes the temptation of Adam, and just as allusively. At the end of the work, though, Otfrid combined his narrative, exegetical, and lyrical powers in a series of memorable chapters. The description of the day of judgment (V, 19) may be compared with the *Muspilli,* and there is a refrain here, too, stressing the need for a man to be sure of his good deeds when he appears before the judge. Christ appears (V, 20) and the judgment is made (V, 21–22), and three chapters follow. The first is concerned with the joys of heaven, and the refrain is a prayer—or rather, two prayers, separate four-line refrains used at frequent intervals in a chapter of nearly three hundred lines. The first prayer is found seven times:

> Biscírmi uns, druhtin gúato   thero selbun árabeito,
>   líchamon joh sela,   in thínes sélbes era;
> Thuruh thíno guati   dúa uns thaz gimúati,
>   wir mit ginádon thinen   thesa árabeit bimíden!   (V, 23, 11–14)

(Shield us, good Lord, from the sufferings / to body and soul, in your own name, / in your goodness be merciful to us, / that we, through grace, may avoid suffering.)

This is a kind of variation on the Kyrie. The second refrain is found fourteen times; it asks fervently for entry into Paradise:

> Thára leiti, drúhtin,   mit thínes selbes máhtin
>   zi thémo sconen líbe   thie holdun scálka thine,
> Thaz wir thaz mámmunti   in thínera munti
>   níazen uns in múate   in éwon zi gúate!   (V, 23, 27–30)

(Lead us there, O Lord, through your power, / to the blessed life, all your beloved servants, / that we may enjoy salvation in your hands / and enjoy it forever.)

This is, in a sense, the theme of the whole work. It is a narrative of the life of Christ, but its commentary points out at all times the reason for the incarnation: so that man can return to Paradise. The final chapters are both prayerlike (V, 24 is headed *Oratio,* "Prayer"), and the concluding section ends with what is almost a refrain. The lines have appeared with a variation just before, and they make an appropriate conclusion:

> Si gúallichi thera énsti   thiu mir thés io giónsti,
>   lób ouh thera giwélti   ána theheinig énti,
> In érdu joh in hímile,   in ábgrunte joh hiar nídere,
>   mit éngilon joh mánnon   in éwinigen sángon! Amen.   (V, 25, 101–4)

(May the beauty of your grace be ever over me, / praise of your power ever without end, / on earth and in heaven, in the depths here below, / with angels and men in eternal song. Amen.)

Thus we are taken back to the chapter with which the work opened, with the need to sing the praise of God in Frankish. At the end, that song unites the men and the angels.

Otfrid owes much to Latin tradition, in form and in content. But he remains the real innovator in German precisely for the reason that his great work is *not* in Latin. With Otfrid's life and passion of Christ, Old High German is brought into world literature.[15] It has been fashionable to dismiss Otfrid as pedestrian; but his poetic achievement is by no means slight, and concentration on the structure and layout of his work—the manuscript being for him the absolute text—reveals how skillfully he pursued his aim of singing the praise of God in Frankish.

Chapter Eight
Devotional Lyrics

A number of small rhymed pieces may be grouped together in view of their religious content. Some of them may be linked directly with the *Evangelienbuch,* and in some cases arguments have even been put forward for a chronological priority over Otfrid, although in no instance has the evidence been conclusive. This does not confirm Otfrid as the originator of rhymed verse in German, but he does remain by a very large margin the first poet to have used rhyme to a major extent, and his work provides a formal yardstick against which these smaller pieces may be set. However brief, these works are all examples of deliberate poetic composition, and are not comparable with, say, glossed versions of Latin hymns.

The Rhymed Prayers

The closest link with Otfrid is found in the two pairs of long-lines, in the Bavarian dialect, added at the end of the Freising copy of the *Evangelienbuch,* which was made at the beginning of the tenth century on the instructions of Bishop Waldo. The scribe, whose name is found with that of Waldo in a Latin couplet, was Sigihart, and the German verses are ascribed to him, even though there is no real evidence for his authorship. *Sigihart's Prayers* (MSD XV, St. XX, Lb. XXXVIII/2) are simple requests, first to God and then to Christ, for mercy. The phrases are all mirrored in Otfrid's work, and may be compared with his version of the Lord's Prayer (II, 21, 27–40) or with other prayers in the *Evangelienbuch* (such as V, 24).

Two similar but later works, in Rhenish and Middle Franconian, respectively, are based on Latin originals. The first, known because of its manuscript provenance as the *Augsburg Prayer* (MSD XIV, St. XVIII, Lb. XXXVII), asks, in four long-lines, that God's grace might free us from the chains of sin. It adapts an early Latin prose prayer (which precedes it in the manuscript) now used in the Litany of the Saints ("O God, whose nature and property is ever to have mercy and to forgive"). The translation was probably made after the end of the ninth century. The second dates from the eleventh century and is found in a manuscript from Trier. This time the German adapts into verse a short passage from Gregory the Great's *Moral Interpretation of the Book of Job,* a very widely read medieval text. Once again the German version is preceded by the Latin in the manuscript. The *Trier Gregory-Poem* (St. LXXXI) is not really a prayer, but rather a statement that the devil should not be feared, as he cannot harm man unless God permits him to do so. The verse is not particularly skilled, especially in the metrical balance.

The Cologne Inscription

Two long-lines forming a strophe very like Otfrid's have been seen as evidence for the use of rhyme before the *Evangelienbuch.* In reconstructed form they read: "Hir maht thu lernan Guld bewervan / Welog inde wi*s*duom Sig*ilof inde ruom*" ("Here you may learn to gain gold, wealth, wisdom, praise and fame") (Lb. IV/1). That the lines are reconstructed— the italics represent conjecture—needs stressing. They once formed an inscription on a building in Cologne, and were copied in a distorted form in 1571 by the geographer Gerard Mercator, who used a set of inscriptions to decorate a map of the city.[1] The Middle Franconian verses were not published until the 1930s. From their position in Mercator's map, it seems possible that the lines were carved over the entrance to the cathedral school or library (with "gold" referring to spiritual riches), and the text may echo II Chronicles 1:12, which refers to God's gifts to Solomon; but the ideas are fairly commonplace, and could also be linked with a number of Latin verses.

The date of the German lines remains a problem. They have been linked with the building of a cathedral library by Bishop Gunthar between 850 and 860, but to conclude from this that the lines predate Otfrid demands the assumption that the inscription was cut when the building was erected, and also that Otfrid—whose dedications we know were written between 863 and 871—wrote none of his Gospel-poem before that time. Almost certainly Otfrid was composing before the Cologne piece was written, and in any case the survival of one single rhymed line and the fragments of a second is slender evidence on which to base a theory of pre-Otfridian rhymed verse.

The Song to St. Peter

Similar problems of chronology have diverted attention from the real points of interest in the Bavarian *Petruslied* [The Song to St. Peter] (MSD

IX, St. XXI, Lb. XXXIII). Here, three two-line strophes are each followed by the refrain "Kyrie eleison, Christe eleison" ("Lord have mercy, Christ have mercy"), the Greek formula still used in the Mass. The first two strophes describe the power given to St. Peter to save men and to admit them to heaven. The last asks us to implore Peter, the beloved of God, to intercede for sinful men.

The Latin manuscript at the end of which the poem has been added is again from Freising. Just above the German is a Latin sentence reading "God the almighty will weigh up their deeds," and this seems to have a loose thematic link with the poem. The name Suonhart is written a little above the German, but whether there is a connection remains unclear.[2]

The *Petruslied* is a song. The text is provided throughout with neumes, an early system of notation that gives an approximate idea of melody.[3] The tune seems to be a fairly complicated one, and the question naturally arises of how and where the work was sung. An attractive suggestion is that it was used by pilgrims on the way to St. Peter's city of Rome, but there is no real evidence for this. The song does seem to have been composed for liturgical reasons, however. While not a translation, it has close parallels with a Latin hymn to St. Peter which is used as a processional on the feast of SS. Peter and Paul on 29 June and which was also used on pilgrimages.[4]

The Kyrie refrain looks very much like a response. The final strophe begins with *bittemes* ("let us implore"), and the Kyrie follows naturally as an answer, but the neumes indicate that this part, too, would have been quite difficult to sing. It is less likely that the response would have been sung by a congregation, then.[5] The use of the Kyrie in vernacular religious songs is not uncommon. Indeed, an abridged form of the word *eleison—leis*—came to be a generic term for later religious songs. The *Petruslied* is, however, a remarkably early example of the use of the Kyrie.

How early is the work? The manuscript can be dated between 850 and 875, and the poem was added later in an early tenth-century hand. The final German line, however, is identical with one in Otfrid. Which came first, or is the line simply a well-known formula? As such, the line is not particularly memorable, and it is found in a formal context—the two-line strophe—closely parallel to that of the *Evangelienbuch*. The rhyme, though, is better in the *Petruslied*, and looks as if it has been polished up. The short poem contains other echoes of the *Evangelienbuch*, however. The part containing the *Petruslied* line (which is significantly near the beginning, I, 7, 25–28) refers to St. John as "the beloved of the Lord," and just before this is a general "let us implore," although with a different verb. It seems likely that the *Petruslied*, like Sigihart's Prayers, depends on the copying of the *Evangelienbuch* at Freising.

Psalm 138

In another manuscript originally from Freising we find a German rhymed adaptation of Psalm 138 (139 in the Protestant tradition; MSD XIII, St. XXII, Lb. XXXVIII).[6] Once again the dialect is Bavarian and the date of composition probably the early tenth century. The formal influence of Otfrid's work seems clear, but the poem really has more in common with the devotional pieces already examined. The adaptation of the Psalm is free, but there are few exegetical additions. Otfrid, too, is telling a story. The German *Psalm 138* retains the character of the original as a song of praise.

The Psalm itself is obscure in places, but there are several clear themes. A statement of God's complete control (vv. 1–6) is developed into an acknowledgment of divine omnipresence (vv. 7–12). A third section returns to God's all-embracing knowledge (vv. 13–18) and the singer then attacks the enemies of God (vv. 19–22). The last two verses ask God to examine the righteousness of the singer. The German adaptation contains most of these ideas, and it is the stress on the totality of God's power over man that must have occasioned the work. The German poem does not, however, follow the biblical order, except at the beginning. The thirty-eight long-lines are grouped in Otfridian couplets for the most part, but there are four three-line strophes, which may have a structural significance. Three individual lines, finally, are repeated in the course of the German poem.

The opening places the Psalm itself into context, with a clear Christian distancing: "Would you hear the deep thoughts of David the good, how he greeted his Lord?" The following five couplets (3–12) keep close to the first six verses of the Psalm, although one change is made: in the German poem God directs the horse, rather than the path, of the singer, who has, as it were, been mounted on horseback. There then follows the first triplet (13–15), rendering verse 8 of the Psalm and stressing God's presence everywhere. The last long-line of the triplet (which is repeated later) is a kind of summary.

Now, however, there comes a clear break in the pattern. Lines 16–24, three couplets and a triplet, adapt verses 19–22 of the original, the passage concerned with God's enemies. The triplet, which is again rather like a summary, adds another new idea: that God should prevent the enemies from shooting their arrows. This idea could well have been borrowed from other biblical passages, though. Of greater interest here is the second of the repetitions, this time two adjacent lines (17 and 18), which make a nonbiblical reference to evil men who may advise the singer to act in a corrupt manner. If we recall at this point that King David is speaking, and that he has been referred to as "the good," just as Otfrid referred to Lewis the Pious, then we may suspect a reference to an aspect of medieval kingship.

Although the couplets which follow (25–28) adapt verses 13–15 of the Psalm, it seems from this point almost as if the translation were being made in reverse. Two couplets and a triplet (29–35) translate first vv. 11–12, then vv. 9–10 of the original. The earlier summarizing line 15 reappears as line 35, and lines 32 and 33 are identical. A concluding triplet adapts the supplication at the end of the biblical text.

Several problems arise: of the repetitions, of the order, and of the nonbiblical ideas. For the first of these problems, the repeat of line 15 can be accepted, but the other two lines do look rather like dittography, the accidental repetition in a manuscript of a word or group of words. Their deletion does not, however, clarify the balance of two- and three-line strophes, and the mixture, which will be encountered again, must be accepted. The question of order is more involved, and since no definite solution is likely to be found, both sides of the case must be stated. Critics have argued both for radical rearrangement and for acceptance of the manuscript order. The former viewpoint is supported by the closeness of the first part of the German work to the original, and would place after lines 1–15 first lines 32–35, then 29–30, 25–28, 16–24, and then 36–38.[7] This does, of course, beg the question of how the text came to be in such disorder. The surviving manuscript gives us no clues, and it is difficult to imagine a situation which would lead to such a copy.

If, on the other hand, we accept that the German poet is adapting with deliberate freedom, then we may divide the poem into three sections, each with a climactic triplet: the first deals with God's omniscience (1–15), the second with the enemies (16–24), and the last with God's knowledge once again (25–35). The final prayer (36–38) rounds off the whole. That the poet adds ideas from other sources supports the concept of a free reworking of the biblical ideas. They do tend to make the poem more vivid—the guiding of the horse, the arrows, and the potential abuse of kingly power. What the German omits is the stress in verse 16 of the Psalm on God's knowledge of the singer before his birth. In the main, though, difficult ideas are well handled, and the result is satisfactory as poetry, even with the repetitions and a use of rhyme which is sometimes unskilled:

so uuillih danne file fruo	stellen mino federa:
peginno ih danne fliogen	sose er netete nioman.
Peginno ih danne fliogen	sose er tete nioman,
so fliugih ze enti ienes meres:	ih uueiz daz du mih dar irferist;
nemegih in nohhein lant,	nupe mih hapet din hant. (31–35)

(Then I shall set my pinions very early, / I begin to fly as no man has ever done. / I begin to fly as no man has ever done, / and I fly to the ends of that far sea: I know you will reach me there; / I may go to no other land unless your hand hold me.)

The totality of divine power is stressed even more clearly than in the original. In the Psalm, God's power is a passive absolute. In the German poem, the power is more dynamic: God will guide, advise, and protect.[8]

Chapter Nine
Rulers and Saints

Lewis of France and the Battle of Saucourt

In comparison with the state of the surviving texts of the *Hildebrandslied* or the *Muspilli,* the *Ludwigslied* [Lay of King Lewis] has been preserved in a clear hand and set out as verse, with capitals indicating a division into strophes of two or three Otfridian long-lines (MSD XI, St. XVI, Lb. XXXVI). The poem was intended as a literary work aimed for posterity, then, but even so, it presents a number of problems. The main subject of the codex in which it is found is a Latin translation of the writings of a Greek theologian. At the end, and in a different hand, is the *Ludwigslied,* but immediately before it, in the same hand, is one of the earliest works known in Old French, the *Song of St. Eulalia.* Just before the French poem we find two Latin poems, one on the same saint, and at the very end of the manuscript some Latin distichs.[1]

The codex is now in Valenciennes, in northern France, but it came from a monastery at St. Amand sur l'Elnon, now just below the Franco-Belgian border. If not the whole manuscript, then at least the vernacular poems were written down in St. Amand, and the *Ludwigslied* is the sole German element in a manuscript from what may be called a French monastery. The content of the poem complicates the matter further. It deals with the victory of King Lewis III of the west Franks—of France—over the Vikings at Saucourt in Picardy in 881. Only the language connects the work with Germany in any way.

The *Ludwigslied* is an historical poem. It narrates events of contemporary history, and also explains them, within a theocentric framework and in a poetically satisfying manner. There are two distinct themes: the life of King Lewis and the Viking attacks on France. The themes come together in the defeat of the Vikings by Lewis at Saucourt.

As previously stated, Charlemagne's empire had been divided on the death of his son, Lewis the Pious, in 840, into three parts. Taking

Charlemagne and his son into account for the regnal numberings, Charles II, the Bald, ruled what we may call France, Lewis II, the German, became king of Germany, and Lothar held the imperial title. Lewis the German was succeeded in 876 by his son, as Lewis III of Germany, and in 877 Charles the Bald was followed on the French throne by *his* son, Lewis II of France. He, however, died after only two years, leaving the western kingdom to his two sons, Lewis III of France, and his brother, Carloman, both of whom were probably still in their teens. Their youth encouraged others to threaten their security as rulers of France. Lewis III of Germany was interested, as was Boso, Duke of Provence, who had married into the family of Lothar, and had taken the title of King of Arles. Nevertheless, the young kings found sufficient support to establish their rule, in spite of ecclesiastical opposition from the powerful Hincmar, archbishop of Rheims. In fact, both kings died young, Carloman in 884 and Lewis as early as 882, and the kingdom (and later the empire) passed ultimately to their half-brother Charles III, known as Charles the Simple.

At this period, the Vikings were enjoying a period of great expansion. The Scandinavian warriors whose maritime efforts had taken, or would take, them to Russia, Africa, Greece, and west to England, Ireland, and ultimately Greenland and America, had begun to attack England in the late eighth century, and they went on doing so for much of the ninth. They were defeated, however, at Edington in 878, meeting strong resistance on the part of King Aelfred the Great. In 886 a formal division of lands between the Saxons and the Vikings—the setting up of the Danelaw—was made in England. The resistance in England, however, encouraged the Vikings to increase their raids in continental Europe. They concentrated on the mouths of the Scheldt and the Somme, and by 880–881 a Viking army had set up winter quarters at Kortrijk, near Ghent. The annals and chronicles of neighboring monasteries report fully, and sometimes luridly, on the raids. All this meant that the young King Lewis, ruler of the northern part of France, was threatened by invaders from the north, just as his brother Carloman was under pressure in the south from Boso of Provence. The brothers combined forces to defeat Boso in 881, and then Lewis returned north, attacking the Vikings unexpectedly at Saucourt on 3 August 881 and defeating them decisively. Apart from the element of surprise, the key to the victory is perhaps found in the Anglo-Saxon chronicle, which shows no interest in Lewis, but does note that the Vikings began after this battle to develop their cavalry. Presumably the French cavalry proved superior against a force used to swift infantry attack, and a return to their boats.

The annals of the monasteries paint a vivid picture of the Viking raids. Those from St. Vaast, south of Ghent, describe the Northmen as burners of churches, eager for devastation, and thirsting for human blood. The same chronicles, predictably enough, rejoice in the victory, and all of them (apart from that under the control of Hincmar) stress the valor of the young king. From the chronicles we may obtain a certain amount of factual information—the date and the place of battle—and some comments, such as the attribution of the victory to God, and indeed the idea that the Vikings had been sent as a kind of punishment. There are no details of the battle as such, although the Vikings certainly did not attack Lewis again.[2] He died, however, almost exactly one year later, and within thirty years Charles the Simple had had to grant the Northmen the land which still bears their name, Normandy. Lewis's death in 882 enables us to date the poem, since he is spoken of as still alive, even though a Latin heading indicates that by the time the work was written down, he was already dead. The manuscript was probably written quite soon after the events, however.

The poem falls into several sections. The first (1–8) introduces the king, noting his piety, and telling how the fatherless youth was cared for by God himself, who provided him with a strong following and a throne. At this point, the poet introduces an exhortatory "long may he reign!"— indicating that the king was at the time of writing still alive. Next we are told how Lewis shared all these benefits with Carloman. The second main section (9–19) turns to the Vikings. God has sent these "heathen men" across the sea for two reasons: to test the mettle of the young king and to admonish the Franks—his people—for their sins, some of which the poet enumerates. Some of the Franks survived, while others did not. Some repented and reformed. The Viking attack, then, is a scourge, inflicted by an angry God, and it is made worse by the absence of the king.

At length, however, God's anger abates, and the king can return (20–28). God speaks to him directly, asking that he return to help "God's people." The king agrees to do so if he is spared, and rides back under a war-banner against the Northmen. His subjects welcome him, and he makes a speech of comfort (29–41): God has sent him back, and although life and death are in the hands of Christ, he, Lewis, will reward any men who follow him, and should they fall, he will recompense their relatives. The attack begins (42–54), and the Franks, headed by Lewis, praise God and sing the Kyrie as they go into battle. They fight with vigor, especially Lewis, and "pour a bitter drink for their enemies." The concluding lines (55–59) praise God and the saints for the fact that Lewis was victorious.

There are some details in the poem that are not found in the chronicles: the eagerness of the Franks for battle, the fact that they missed the absent king, and the singing of the Kyrie. Other details are added, such as the divine inspiration of Lewis's return. On the other hand, there are omissions. The place and time of the battle are missing, and so is the reason why Lewis was away. The major difference between the chronicle reports and the poem, however, lies in the presentation of the events. In the *Ludwigslied* there is a complete and consistent integration of event and interpretation. The events of 880 and 881 are set in an ordered economy of history, and we are shown not only the facts, but also the reasons behind them as the poet-historian perceives them.

The poem shares with (most of) the chronicles a stress on the king's bravery. This is to be expected, but it has been suggested that this stress indicates a political purpose behind the poem, emphasizing for the West Frankish nobility, perhaps in direct opposition to Hincmar, that Lewis had the support of God.[3] The poem may well be a propaganda piece. At the same time, the historiography is interesting. The poet sees God as being in control of human events, arranging them in a manner which may be discernible to the objective observer. At the same time, however, the poet is aware that the participants in an historical event cannot know the outcome in advance. Some men, however (like those of the Franks who repent their evil ways under the Viking onslaught) may be able to grasp the divine purpose behind otherwise unpleasant happenings. The poet of the *Ludwigslied* distinguishes well between historical narrative and overall interpretation. The desire to set Saucourt into a framework, too, has dictated his historical selectivity. Thus there is no mention of Boso, the reason for Lewis's absence. Boso, while condemned as a usurper, was still a Christian, and reference to him might have detracted from the theocentric approach. The date and the place are not there simply because this is a poem and not an historical record, but they are in any case of secondary importance. Others will record the date—as indeed they did. The poem is concerned with interpretation. Smaller details, such as the singing of the Kyrie (which is recorded in chronicles about other battles) may, in fact, be historical.

The poet-narrator has a dominant role, which contrasts sharply with the narrator of the *Hildebrandslied*. There the self-effacing speaker had "heard tell" only of the events narrated. Here the speaker "knows a king," is well informed about his childhood, and comments throughout on the action. The older poet let his characters speak for themselves.

To claim that "God is the hero of the *Ludwigslied*," however, is to oversimplify the poem. God, after all, sends the Vikings in the first place. The victory is not God's victory, but Lewis's victory for God's reasons. Unlike the chroniclers, the poet does not characterize the Vikings. They do not thirst for blood. The poet knows why they have been sent, and, as they are merely instruments of God's purpose, there is no point in censuring, or even characterizing, them. They are simply "heathen men."

The notion of the "scourge of God" is an Old Testament one, as is the notion of "God's people," which is also voiced in our poem. Nebuchadnezzar is described as a servant of God (since he is sent to punish the Jews) in Jeremiah 25:8–9, and similar passages may be adduced. Later on, both Alexander the Great and Attila come to be described as a scourge wielded by God. In the *Ludwigslied* the Vikings achieve their double objective: the men mend their ways, and Lewis is tested in battle. But while doing God's work, he behaves as a credible worldly ruler. He admits that the outcome of battle is in God's hands, even if he does promise recompense and rewards. He does not, incidentally, promise a place in heaven to the fallen: that too is God's affair. The singing of the Kyrie is significant: "Lord have mercy on us" is an expression of submission to the divine will, and not a presumption of glory. We may compare the poem briefly with a later poetical tradition about an earlier battle, the defeat of Charlemagne's lieutenant Roland by the Saracens at Roncesvalles in 778. A German poem of the twelfth century portrays Roland on his way into battle, having promised his men a martyr's crown if they fall. Roland's soldiers sing the Gloria, since they, in effect, cannot lose. The poet of the *Ludwigslied* has his Franks, less sure of God's judgment on the individual, sing the Kyrie.

The last lines of the poem typify the dominant parataxis in the style which is so useful in dividing narration from comment:

> Gilobot si thiu godes kraft!   Hluduig uuarth sigihaft,
>   ioh allen heiligon thanc!   Sin uuarth ther sigikamf.   (55f.)

(Praised be the power of God. Lewis was victorious. And thanks to all the saints. His was the victory.)

On the one side there are the facts: Lewis was victorious. On the other there is a generally formulated praise for God, who has arranged everything, even the now-finished tribulation of the Vikings and their raids, for the best.[4] That the battle was in the long term indecisive is irrelevant to an

appreciation of the poem, which was written when the events were fresh
and the king was still young. The Vikings had been beaten back, almost
for the first time, by a Frankish army, and it is understandable that a song
should be made of this.

The poem has been known to scholarship for longer than many of the
Old High German writings, but its history is of some interest. It was
discovered in the seventeenth century, and an inaccurate text was published in 1696, after which the manuscript was lost. The poem caught the
imagination, however, of figures like Herder and Rodmer, and there were
several editions. In 1837, however, the scholar and poet Heinrich
Hoffmann von Fallersleben rediscovered the work in Valenciennes and
printed a text that was nearly correct, although one small linguistic error
remained to cause some confusion until it was clarified fairly recently.[5]
Although the textual problems have now been settled, the problem
remains of the poem's existence in German at all. Indeed, the dialect of the
poem makes things even more complicated. Although the poem was
written and probably composed in St. Amand, the language is Rhenish
Franconian, a dialect which does not touch Romance territory anywhere
near that area.

The authorship is, of course, never likely to be discovered. The suggestion was once made, however, that the poem is by Hucbald, the scholar-
abbot of St. Amand. Since he was claimed as the author of the French
Eulalia and the Latin poems, too, and since none of these is anything like
his correctly attested Latin writings, the suggestion may be dismissed, but
mention of his name reminds us that St. Amand was indeed a center of
learning, and it was known, too, as an aristocratic foundation, which
might have attracted monks of noble background from all parts of Charlemagne's empire. A case has, in fact, been made for the *Ludwigslied* as an
illustration of poetry in a "Carolingian court language" (an analogy with
the use of Norman-French in postconquest England), German still spoken
by the Frankish aristocracy even after the adoption of French.[6] Other
evidence for such a court language remains scanty, however, and we have
to accept that the poem was in all probability composed by a speaker of
Rhenish Franconian resident at St. Amand. The poem is unlikely to have
been composed in Germany itself. Why should such a poem concern itself
with a French king, when the German Lewis had himself fought against
the Vikings in 880? The poet, too, was surely a subject of Lewis of France,
keen to support him. There are, in fact, records of other (lost) German
works once in the monastery of St. Amand, and our poem must be counted
a fortunate survival. There is no real connection with the *Eulalia* poem,

although the scribe does seem to have been able to write both French and German well. There are a few Romance features in the German text, but none of any great significance.

Generic discussions of Old High German poems are rarely fruitful in view of the small number of texts that have survived at all. Various comparisons may be made between the *Ludwigslied,* however, and poems in Latin or other languages, specifically to the Latin panegyric on a ruler (or saint), and on the other hand to the Germanic-heroic battle-poem. In the past, critics have tried to see in the poem a simple Christianization of a Germanic epic, although for some the Christian elements were overpowering. Andreas Heusler, for example, spoke derogatorily of the "ecclesiastical puppet-mentality" of the work,[7] a comment which ignores the fact that Lewis and his followers are shown to be unaware of the divine plan in all its detail: they have free choice to carry out God's will or not, and the poet's theology is more consistent and a good deal more orthodox than Heusler's.

The division created by critics in stressing too heavily the Christian or the Germanic aspects has been, as Max Wehrli has pointed out, unproductive. The poem may contain elements that can be linked with the formalized Latin panegyric, and it certainly has features which compare with Old Norse or Anglo-Saxon heroic poems—Lewis's address to his followers before the battle, for example. The phrasing of the battle-scene recalls works of this type, too, but that is only to be expected. The poem may be compared, too, with Christian-Latin poems celebrating, for example, the victory of Pippin, Charlemagne's father, over the Huns. Even here there are differences, however: the Vikings are not criticized in our work in the manner in which the enemies are treated in such Latin poems. The *Ludwigslied* is, finally, in German, and precisely *not* in Latin.[8] The closest parallels with the poem come, in fact, rather later, with the medieval French *chansons de geste,* Christian battle epics. Saucourt itself inspired such a poem, even if the enemy had by then become not Vikings but Saracens. The *Ludwigslied* is nothing more than a forerunner, however, and anachronistic literary designations—"crusading poem" is another—can be dangerous.

It is not without significance that the poem employs the new Otfridian rhyme (although there are three- as well as two-line strophes). Here too, though, the structure of the work and its possible manner of performance continue to present questions that seem to be unanswerable. What remains in the mind is the striking thematic line, the person of the king uniting the events: the work begins with his youth, and ends with a prayer for his life. It progresses smoothly to the testing of the king, and when God's anger has passed, the poet can set up a line of contact from God to Lewis, from Lewis to the Franks, and from the Franks to the Vikings, with decreasing interest in characterization. The battle itself is of limited interest—and this marks a difference from the later *chansons de geste*. What matters is the place of the battle in God's plan. The work is a Christian historical poem. The historiographic framework which subordinates all events to God's direction is long out of fashion. For all that, the *Ludwigslied* is consistent within itself, and as the first original rhymed poem on a secular theme in German, it still remains within the Christian framework of the bulk of Old High German literature.

De Heinrico

Latin poems such as the panegyric on Pippin's victory over the Avar Huns referred to in the context of the *Ludwigslied* have, of course, a claim to be included in the early literary history of Germany. Since such works *are,* however, in Latin, a survey of Old High German writings can do little more than mention them, even though Müllenhoff and Scherer, for example, included in their anthology a number of Latin poems with clear connections with German history. The *Modus Ottinc* [Song of Otto] (MSD XXII) and the *Modus qui et Carelmanninc* [Song Which Is Also Carloman's] (MSD XIX) are two of a series of *modi* with secular rulers as their themes, which come from a collection of forty-nine poems found in a manuscript which is now in Cambridge. The *Cambridge Songs* were copied in England, probably in Canterbury, in the eleventh century, but the original of the collection was German. Among the Latin poems there is one historical piece that is macaronic, written, that is, in a mixture of German and Latin. *De Heinrico* [Of Henry] (MSD XVIII, St. XXIII, Lb. XXXIX) is composed in eight stanzas, the first, second, and fifth with four, the rest with three rhymed long lines, the first half of each line being in Latin, the second half in German. The dialect is Rhenish Franconian, although this may be an adaptation from an original with a different dialect.[9]

The poem begins with a reference to a certain Duke Henry of the Bavarians. In the next strophe, a messenger addresses the emperor Otto, telling him that Henry has arrived with a large and worthy following. Otto receives him with honor, welcoming him in the fourth strophe, and Henry responds, after which he accompanies Otto to Mass. In strophe 6, Henry is again received and given all powers "except the regal one, which Henry did not desire." The two final stanzas tell how Henry then led the council as Otto's principal adviser and praise him in general terms. The penultimate strophe is effective in its form, although the first line mixes the Latin and German parts:

> Tunc stetit al thiu sprakha   sub firmo Heinriche.
> quicquid Otdo fecit,   al geried iz Heinrih;
> quicquid ac omisit,   ouch geried iz Heinrihc. (22–24)

(Then all the council was under the leadership of Henry. / Whatever Otto did, was on the advice of Henry. / What he left undone was on the advice of Henry).

Who, however, are Otto and Henry? The question is made very difficult indeed by the profusion both of Ottos and Henrys in imperial, regal, and ducal roles in the tenth and eleventh centuries. The third strophe of the poem complicates the issue. In welcoming Henry, Otto says, "welcome Henry, both of you of the same name," a comment which has led scholars to search the history books for two Henrys who might have appeared before an emperor named Otto. It seems likely, however, that the stanza is corrupt. It presents extensive linguistic problems in that it seems to be in Old Saxon, and there is, after all, no reference anywhere else in the poem to another Henry, although the central Duke Henry is mentioned by name nine times.

Two possible incidents have been suggested as the basis for the poem. The first takes the emperor to be Otto I, the Great (936–973) and Henry his younger brother, who, after several rebellions, was reconciled with him at Christmas 941 and created Duke of Bavaria. The celebration of Mass would fit into this scheme, and the poem might then have been written during the reign of the later emperor, Henry II, grandson of the first duke of Bavaria, who ruled between 1002 and 1024. There is, it is true, no reference to any reconciliation in the poem, but a retrospective work might very well gloss over such unpleasant details.

An equally good, if not better, case can be made, however, for taking the poem as referring to contemporary events at the end of the tenth century, to the reconciliation between Otto III (983–1002) and Henry the Quarrelsome, second duke of Bavaria, son of the first rebel Henry, and father of the future emperor. Henry the Quarrelsome had been banished by Otto II (973–983), and when Otto III became emperor in 983, at the age of three years, Henry tried to gain the regency. He failed to do so, but was reinstated eventually as duke of Bavaria, and joined the regent's council in 991. All this would accord with the advice which plays such a part in the poem, and the apparently dominant role of Henry over Otto.

One problem is common to both readings of the story. Otto is referred to as emperor, and if he is Otto I this would be anachronistic. He assumed the title only after Henry of Bavaria had died. Otto III was only crowned emperor after the regency. The title could well have been applied retrospectively, however, and, whichever historical events are treated here, the work is still likely to be a product of the *imperium* of Henry II, making more respectable the deeds either of his quarrelsome father or his rebellious grandfather. As an example of macaronic poetry, the work is effective, with good rhymes and a nice balance in most of the lines. As a macaronic poem, it is likely to have been a kind of clerical exercise, however, and it neither forms part of the Latin panegyric tradition nor links with the historical scale of the *Ludwigslied*.

St. Gall and St. George

Two saints' lives are known to have been composed in German during the Old High German period, but in neither case—although for different reasons—do we know what the original text was like. The first was the work of Ratpert, a monk of St. Gallen, who died toward the end of the ninth century. Basing himself on Latin material, he wrote a metrical German *Life of St. Gall,* the Irish missionary and putative founder of his monastery, who had died in the mid-seventh century. Ratpert's text is lost, but we have a Latin translation of it (with a preface) made by a later monk and chronicler of St. Gallen, Ekkehart IV, who was born about a century after Ratpert's death and died in 1060. He wrote down his version of Ratpert's *carmen barbaricum* himself, and copied it twice more. The German is impossible to reconstruct (it is printed in Latin in MSD XII), but Ekkehart does speak of having retained the melody (which we have), so that the form of the original may be reflected in the Latin. Following Latin hymns, however, Ekkehart uses seventeen five-line strophes, and this would have been unusual in German in Ratpert's day. The style is fairly simple, and this may reflect the original. Each line expresses a single thought, recalling the paratactic style of the *Ludwigslied* and looking ahead to the *Georgslied.* The poem tells of the mission of the Irish monks Columban, Gall, and others to southern Germany and Switzerland. Gall falls ill and is left behind at one point, although forbidden to say Mass until he knows Columban has died. He finds a remote retreat, survives a forest fire, tames a bear (later his symbol), drives off demons, and heals the sick, but refuses to be the spiritual leader of the community which grows up around him. On the death of Columban (told in a vision) he begins to celebrate Mass and works several miracles, although these are too briefly put to be clear without reference to other lives of the saint. When he dies, his disciples find marks of self-inflicted scourging, and his corpse is taken to its resting-place by untamed horses. The final strophe is hymnlike: Gall will live in his miracles and will continue to protect men.

The rather different problems of the *Georgslied* [Song of St. George] (MSD XVII, St. XIX, Lb. XXXV) are immediately apparent from a glance at the text in the *Lesebuch,* where we are offered three versions: the manuscript text, and edited reading versions by Friedrich Zarncke and by Rudolf Koegel, both made in the late nineteenth century. Zarncke divides the fifty-five to sixty long-lines into nine strophes of between five and eight lines, plus an incomplete strophe. Koegel sees the whole work as made up of two- and three-line strophes.[10] One example will make the problem clear. One of St. George's miracles is described as follows: "a pillar had stood for many years, suddenly it produced leaves. / George worked the miracle, in truth." Zarncke prints

> ein sûl stuont dâr manic iâr: ûz spranc der loub sâr.
> Daz zeihhan worhta dâre   Gorio zi wâre.   (20–21, both texts)

Koegel's text is very similar at this point, but the manuscript original is very different indeed. It reads:

> ehin suhl stuonetehr magihe ihar uhus. psanr dher. lob. shar.
> das. zehiken. uuorehta. dhare. gorio ze uuare.

There are no gaps in these lines—as there are elsewhere in the manuscript—but apart from the fact that the dots give no real assistance toward punctuation, the language is even stranger than some of the ciphers used in glosses, the Franco-German of the Paris sentences, or the mixture of the *Hildebrandslied.* Here, *psanr* is a distorted and incomplete form of *spranc,* but the form recurs later. Other distortions appear to be explicable. The word *helle,* for example, appears as *ehtle,* with a curious initial reversal, but a less unusual error in the crossed upright of the *l.* In dialect terms, too, a word like *zehiken* looks as if it had a Low German *k* (English *token,* German *Zeichen*), but elsewhere there are consonant shiftings which look like Upper German. Most perplexing is the use of the letter *h,* following vowels it ought to precede, and appearing where it is entirely uncalled for, between the vowels of a diphthong and even after consonants. The equivalent of modern *Himmelreich* ("heaven") appears as *ihmilrike,* with an *h* written above the *r,* and *rhike* crops up later.

There seems to be a regular system, but it remains a mystery whether the intent is to reflect actual sounds or to provide a kind of code. The text breaks off in the middle of a narrative section with the words "ihn nequeo Vuisolf." Wisolf was probably the scribe's name, and *nequeo* means "I can't do it," "I give up," while *ihn* seems to be the same in German—*ih ne*, "I can't." Perhaps it all became too much for the scribe.

Nevertheless, it is possible to sort out the disorder and put together a reading text. The style of this life of St. George resembles the St. Gall poem in the brief noting of miracles without any real background, although the form is not as regular. The manuscript is no help with the layout, but there are repeated lines, and in one case a three-line repetition. These repeated passages clearly mark major divisions in the work, and tend to confirm Zarncke's strophic pattern.

Where the miracles of St. Gall are essentially pastoral, those of St. George are in the bloodier tradition of the early martyrs, and most of them show the saint surviving repeated attempts to put him to death. St. George may have been a real person, but he is a shadowy saint.[11] Perhaps a Roman soldier, he seems to have been killed during the anti-Christian campaign started in 303 by Galerius, then caesar, or joint ruler, of the eastern Roman empire. Galerius, from Dacia, appears as "King Dacianus" in the legends.

George was a popular saint, and versions of his life exist in numerous languages, telling of his high position, his miracles, and his beheading, although it is not until the thirteenth century that the story of the dragon-slaying comes to be attached to his name. A Latin life from St. Gallen is close to the poem and may have been its source. There is other historical evidence to link the German poem with the Alemannic area. In 888 a church was dedicated to St. George on the Reichenau, and the relics of the saint—supposedly including his head—were brought there in 896. Either occasion could have prompted a German poem. As far as one can tell, the language is Alemannic, and it is likely, then, that the poems of St. Gall and of St. George were composed chronologically and geographically close to one another.

The poem begins *in medias res*. George, a warrior, is to face a tribunal, but we do not know why. He is urged to change his beliefs (although again his Christianity is not stressed), and, asserting that he is "true to God," he is put into prison, where angels serve him, and where he saves the lives of two women. He then heals the sick, the blind, and the lame and makes the pillar come into leaf. This angers Dacianus, who tries to kill George by swords, and on the wheel, and by stoning. The repeated phrase "ûf irstuont sih Gorio dâr" presumably means that he rose unscathed, rather than rose from the dead, although there are some links with Christ. George then raises a dead man, converts the wife of Dacianus, and, in the final, incomplete strophe, banishes a demon.

Wisolf could not go on. Probably not too much is missing from the work, which, compared to parallel versions in other languages, is very succinct.[12] Conceived as part of a specific cult-veneration in the late ninth century, the work was written down about a century later, around 1000, and coincidentally there is more of a connection with Otfrid than the use of rhymed long lines. The manuscript in which it is found is one of the Weissenburg copies of the *Evangelienbuch,* now in Heidelberg, and possibly a dedication copy sent to St. Gallen. The actual script of the poem, on the last pages, while damaged by chemicals, is reasonable clear.[13] It is a pity that the same cannot be said for the language.

Chapter Ten
Some Literary Enigmas

It is difficult in a survey of Old High German writings to know where to draw the line. The fragmented emergence of writings in the German language is underlined with some clarity by the smallest survivals in prose and verse, although these do, it is true, stretch the term "literary" to its limits. Often they are merely flyleaf jottings, marginalia in the literal sense, perhaps just a scribe testing a new pen. All of these pieces combine smallness of size with a quite disproportionate difficulty of interpretation, yet the justification for grouping them together, and indeed for studying them at all, is that they show us people thinking in the vernacular, and may even provide evidence for lost genres in the vernacular. It must be recalled, too, that works like the *Petruslied* are, after all, not so very much bigger than many of these little pieces.

Some of them, on the other hand—especially the secular poetic fragments—have called forth an unparalleled ingenuity on the part of the critics, and great edifices of interpretation have been erected upon a few words of German. So too, although some have been claimed as predating Otfrid in the use of rhyme, chronology here is even more difficult than usual. The fragments collected in this chapter cover a long period of time.

Macaronics

Once again it is impossible to discuss here the Latin poems of the Cambridge manuscript—in this case the comic-satirical pieces which Müllenhoff and Scherer included with the historical poems in their anthology (MSD XX–XXI and XXIII–XXV)—even if these, too, provide evidence of a parallel, but lost, vernacular tradition.[1] We may consider, however, two mixed Latin-German pieces, the first of which is, like the macaronic poem already discussed, *De Heinrico,* also preserved in the Cambridge codex. The work is known from its opening as *Suavissima nunna* [O Sweetest Nun],[2] and it takes the form of a dialogue between an unidentified man and a nun. The man urges the nun to love him, but she resists, although she may perhaps relent at the end of the work. The lines seem to be Latin in the first half, German in the second, with assonance between the halves:

Hoc (euanescit) omne   also (w)olcan in th(emo h)imele

(All these things shall pass like clouds in the sky)

The hypothetical tone of this summary stems from the fact that the work is badly damaged. It was apparently censored in the Middle Ages, the later parts in particular being scratched out, and the chemicals used in nineteenth-century restoration attempts made things worse. The medieval censorship does seem to support the view that the nun eventually gives in, however.

Even in its present state the work is interesting. The use of dialogue points forward to the same technique in love poetry of the high Middle Ages, and the nature imagery of the work is also striking. On the evidence of the form, on the other hand, it looks as if the poem were a clerical product, the work of someone used to Latin models, of which there are examples elsewhere in the Cambridge codex, rather than the survivor of a popular genre.

The second dual-language fragment is even smaller, four German words only in an (incomplete) epic poem containing well over two thousand Latin hexameters. The eponymous hero of the Latin work, *Ruodlieb,* has a German name, and there are other German names in the epic, which probably dates from the latter part of the eleventh century. There are a few German glosses in the sole surviving manuscript, which is from Tegernsee. The epic deals with the exile and return of a nobleman, Ruodlieb, who at one point seeks a wife (who turns out to be less virtuous than she seems). The hero sends her a declaration of love, to which she replies using a very stylized rhetorical formula. She has for Ruodlieb "as much *love* as the trees have *leaves* / and as much *delight* as the birds give, so much *love* as that."[3] The Latin lines have internal rhyme, and in the lines cited (which are repeated in the work) the rhyme words—here italicized—are in German. Why these German words should appear in this moralizing episode (Ruodlieb indicates his knowledge of the lady's past, and she decides not to marry) is not clear, but the use of rhyme words in German may be evidence of other rhymed love-poetry here adapted to suit a rhetorical topos. Slender though it is, this may be the only evidence

we have of a love-song tradition in Old High German, although it is worth
noting that as early as 789 a legal document proscribes *uuinileodos,* which
may mean "love-songs."

Prose

Fragments of secular prose that might be seen as a close reflection of
spoken Old High German are rare, and sometimes close to glosses. At the
end of a manuscript of the early eleventh century containing parts of the
Dialogues of St. Gregory the Great a scribe writes in Latin and then in
German: *"Explicit liber tertius dialogorvm* ["Here ends the third book of
Dialogues"]. That means the speech of two, for two are speaking all this. I
mean, one asks the questions and the other answers" (St. LXXXVII).
Other pieces are equally clearly *not* connected with the manuscript in
which they are found. Steinmeyer's anthology includes a few such pieces
(St. LXXXII/1 cites a marginal note), and these are often shakily written
in, or partially erased from, the manuscripts. Steinmeyer's last piece (St.
LXXXVIII), which he calls a *Federprobe* ("Testing the Pen"), looks more
than anything like a shopping-list or an *ad hoc* reminder. Money is
mentioned, and something has been sent to Thuringia. . . . The rest is
unintelligible.

More rewarding are the surviving Old High German proverbs. A St.
Gallen codex contains two: "When it rains, the trees get wet, and when it
blows, the trees sway" and "When the roebuck runs away, you can see his
white backside" (St. LXXXVI). The former is used by Notker Labeo
(whose own work will be discussed in the next chapter) as an illustration of
inevitability in a tract on logic. He does not include the roebuck proverb,
yet both were, presumably, familiar sayings in his day. Notker in fact cites
a series of proverbs (MSD XXVII, Lb. XXIII/18), of which at least one is
more remarkable than those cited above: "If man is to fear all the beasts,
then he should fear none more so than man."

Verse

Some of the poetic survivals are equally small. A single rhymed long
line of the ninth century is found in full in one, in part in another St.
Gallen manuscript. It has been claimed that the line "affords a glimpse
into the everyday life of the ever-occupied monks of the scriptorium,"[4] and
it reads: "I have written with great effort, and with even greater effort I
have been waiting for this moment" (MSD XVb, St. LXXXIII). This sort

of thing is often found at the end of a manuscript, although in neither of the St. Gallen versions is it actually found in that position. It may be a scriptorium tag used as writing practice.

Manuscripts from the same monastery preserve two other small pieces, a single rhymed long line and a couplet. The former is known in a corrupt form in the margin of an eleventh-century codex, then, in rather clearer form, a few pages later, also in the margin. The line seems to mean: "The stranger from Chur [in Raetia, hence a speaker of Italian or of Romansch?] came here, to the land where streets are paved with gold" (MSD XXVIII/ 1, St. LXXXII/1). The verse may refer to a local incident, but it is interesting that the metrical form is highly polished.[5] The other St. Gallen piece is more clearly intended as a lampoon. It is earlier than the first, written in about 900 on the front leaf of a Vulgate Bible, together with some Latin oddments and drawings. The *St. Galler Spottvers* [St. Gallen Lampoon] tells how "Liubwin set out the beer, and gave his daughter away. / But then Starzfidere turned up and brought his daughter back" (MSD XXVIII/2, St. LXXXII/2). The situation appears—from the beer—to be a rustic one, perhaps a wedding or betrothal. Starzfidere is a humorous name, meaning perhaps "Ass-feathers," or possibly something more obscene, playing on the notion "cock." The return of the daughter is likely to have been ignominious, but the reasons for her rejection are not given. A plausible suggestion is that she is being returned after marriage on grounds of infertility. This may be a survival of folk-poetry, but its preservation on a St. Gallen Vulgate is very odd indeed.[6]

The one and a half long lines known as *Hirsch und Hinde* [Hart and Hind] (MSD VI, St. LXXIX) may also be a relic of popular poetry. It is usually (but not always) assumed that this is a fragment, and the fact that the complete long line both rhymes and alliterates make metrical analysis difficult. Once again the text is found in the margin of a St. Gallen manuscript, in an eleventh-century hand, with musical notation. The text reads: "The hart whispered into the hind's ear, / 'Will you, hind?'" Some highly imaginative interpretations have been suggested. The lines have been seen as a proverb, as a hunting ritual, as the fragment of an historical epic, and as an erotic song. At opposite extremes it has been linked with Germanic fertility dances and seen (by Gustav Ehrismann in an unusually far fetched section of his literary history) as part of a long allegory with a moral point against concupiscence.[7] The nine surviving words can barely support any of these views, and a convincing explanation is still wanting.

Equally imaginative and varied have been the views on some German verses used once again by Notker Labeo, this time to illustrate points in a

Latin rhetorical handbook, two couplets and a triplet of long lines in rhyme (MSD XXVI, Lb. XL). The preservation is good in this case, because there are several manuscripts of Notker's work, and since Notker is presumably quoting verses well known to him, we may date them to the mid-tenth century or earlier. The verses do present an immediate problem, though, in that it is unclear whether we are dealing with one, two, or three poems. Notker separates them, but the second couplet and the triplet share a theme—the description of a boar.

As with the proverbs, Notker is using German material known to him to illustrate a point. The two couplets illustrate the use in rhetoric of plays with sound. A Latin example (from Vergil) is followed by the first German couplet, describing the clashing of two warriors. After the word *item* (another example) comes a verse which tells how "The boar goes along the mountain-side, a spear in his side. / His great strength does not let him fall." This illustrates the use of sound, then, the crashing of the giant boar. Later on comes the German triplet, but this illustrates hyperbole, exaggeration, and again it is about a boar, whose "feet are the size of a cart, / his bristles high as a forest, / and his tusks twelve ells in length."

The first couplet looks like a fragment of heroic poetry. In spite of the rhyme, there are strong alliterative elements, too. The two pieces about the boar have been the object of much speculation, especially by critics who take them as part of one poem. They have been seen as a simple "tall story," as the reflection of a real event, as a hunting piece, as a riddle, or as a celebration of the founding of a castle at Ebersberg (Boar Mountain). Two extremes are represented in this case by the linking of the boar on the one hand with the giant Calydonian boar described by Ovid in his *Metamorphoses*—which would make the piece into "learned" poetry—and on the other with Gullinborsti, the boar associated in northern mythology with the god Frey.[8] Both views are arguable, and, as so often before, no definite solution is likely to be found. What is of interest is that Notker should use these fragments of German verse as illustrations in a learned Latin context.

Dubia

As we have seen with the Cambridge songs, Latin pieces can often lead us to suspect lost genres, and indeed specific works in German. Müllenhoff and Scherer printed a *Spielmannsreim* ("Minstrel Rhyme") (MSD VIII) which is, in fact, only a confident reconstruction from Latin verse of what *may* have been a German original, although the title given to it is well-nigh meaningless. There are good grounds for assuming German originals for the riddle, attested in our period in Latin, of the "featherless bird" (a snowflake), since the Latin translates so easily into alliterative German verse, and for the well-known poem about the Kölbigk dancers (condemned to dance forever for their impiety). Other, similar cases might be adduced.[9] An interesting final example is provided by the somewhat different case of the Old High German *Schlummerlied* [Lullaby]. In this case a German text exists, but there is doubt about its authenticity. The poem (in a mixture of rhyme and alliteration) invokes pagan goddesses and possibly Wodan himself, "the one-eyed Lord, who will give you [the child being rocked to sleep] hard spears." The piece was discovered in the last century on a manuscript scrap containing material in Hebrew, and has been generally assumed to be a forgery. As a result, it rarely appears in anthologies or literary histories. It cannot yet be restored to them, but palaeographic analysis may eventually establish whether the text is genuine or not. If it is, then the by now very familiar range of interpretative difficulties will arise. If not, it will leave behind a century of controversy and also a certain amount of regret.[10]

Chapter Eleven

Notker Labeo
and the
Later Prose Writings

Notker

Prose writing in German in the late tenth and early eleventh centuries is dominated by Notker Labeo, a monk and teacher at St. Gallen. A large body of material, mainly translations and commentaries, has survived, illustrating not only the language and translation techniques of the time, but also the educational methods. The monastery school at St. Gallen was founded in the eighth century and soon became famous. The monks to whom Otfrid made his final dedication taught here, as did Ratpert, and, much later, the translator of his *Galluslied,* Ekkehart IV, Notker's pupil. An earlier namesake, Ekkehart I, composer of the Latin epic *Waltharius,* taught at St. Gallen, too. The school catered to Benedictine novices, and also to secular pupils, largely the sons of noblemen. It taught the rudiments, then the seven liberal arts: (Latin) grammar, rhetoric, and dialectic, and after that arithmetic, music (for liturgical performance), geometry, and astronomy (which might include basic geography as well). The ultimate aim was the proper understanding of theology, and the basic catechetical texts would come early, too, followed by biblical books like the Psalms, studied, translated, and expounded. Other textbooks known at St. Gallen include a variety of classical and postclassical Latin works, such as the *Marriage of Philology and Mercury,* an allegory by the fifth-century writer Martianus Capella, in which Philology, married to the god of eloquence, is attended by the liberal arts. Equally popular as a school text in the Middle Ages was the *Consolation of Philosophy,* by Boethius, a statesman and scholar put to death in 524, who also translated and commented on some of the works of Aristotle. Two of these, the *Categories* and the *Hermeneutics,* were also known in St. Gallen. All of these works were translated and discussed by Notker.

Three monks of St. Gallen bore the name. Notker I (ca. 840–912), known as Balbulus ("Stammerer"), was a Latin poet of some importance both to letters and to music, and his writings tell us much about the educational program of the school. Notker II, who died in 975, was a physician, whose well-attested disciplinarian severity earned him the name Piperisgranum ("Peppery"). Notker III was born in the mid-tenth century, and acquired the names Labeo ("Thick-lipped") and Teutonicus ("The German," from his writings). He seems to have come from a noble Alemannic family, and was respected inside and outside St. Gallen. He died of the plague on 29 June 1022 and was buried with three colleagues, also victims.

Notker explains his work in a letter written to Hugo, bishop of Sion, in the Valais, in southern Switzerland. In this letter, Notker affirms, first of all, the need for monks to be able to read theological texts. To overcome the difficulties presented by these Latin writings, however, Notker tells Hugo that he has attempted "something almost unknown": the translation of basic works into German. The letter lists his translations, including Boethius, Martianus Capella, and the Psalter, as well as a number of lost works, including Vergil's *Georgics,* a play by Terence, and the book of Job. Notker also names several Latin works of his, including a manual of rhetoric. Any or all of these Notker is prepared, he says, to make available to Hugo, provided the latter sends him sufficient parchment and money for the copying. Although Hugo might find the idea unfamilar at first, he should endeavor on reading them to "think me present." One can indeed conjure up Notker at work from a study of the writings.[1]

The final part of the letter concerns an exchange of manuscripts among Sion, St. Gallen, and the Reichenau, but just before this Notker adds a few remarks on German as a useful aid to understanding the Latin. He also comments briefly, but does not elaborate, on the need to provide German with accents. Like Otfrid, Notker thinks of himself as an innovator. But while he is much concerned with language as such—nearly all his works are concerned with rhetoric—his ultimate aim remains the teaching of reading and composition in Latin. The championship of German, however forceful, is only a means to an end.

Notker does indeed use accents in his writing of German, an acute accent for stress, a circumflex for long vowels. He also regularizes German orthography in his use of an "Initial Consonant Rule" (*Anlautgesetz*), which affects the writing of *b, g,* and *d* (when it represents a sound deriving from a Germanic *th*-). The consonants are written in these forms only when the word immediately preceding ended in a vowel, a liquid, or a nasal (*l, r, m, n*). Other cases—such as the beginning of sentences or clauses, where there is nothing preceding—call for the unvoiced sounds *p*, *k*, and *t* instead. Thus Notker will write "fóne *d*îen *d*íngen" but "*t*és ist óuh *t*úrft" ("from these things," "it is also necessary"). Not all the manuscripts are consistent, but this orthographic rule is found widely.[2]

Notker tackled various difficult translations, and his German vocabulary is large, containing many words not previously attested, and which he may have coined. In any case, he tries hard to make his meaning clear by contextual variation: the word *ecclesia* might be rendered in up to a dozen different ways. His use of abstract formations is also noteworthy, and a large percentage of words first attested in Notker survive into the later stages of the language. Sometimes the translations are striking. The complicated idiom of Psalm 136:6 ("let my tongue cleave to my jaws") is neatly simplified as "stúm uuerde ih" ("I shall become dumb"), for example. In other cases, however, Notker stays closer to his original. Frequently his German is not really German at all, but an artificial mixture of German and Latin, with Latin elements left untranslated that frequently bear the weight of the sense. These would, of course, be the most important words for the pupil to learn, would have been expounded in class, and hence are left untranslated as a deliberate pedagogical strategy. To take a second illustration from the Psalter, Notker translates Psalm 76:8 ("will God then cast off forever") as "Feruuírfet Got zegetâte *genus humanum*" ("does God cast away the *genus humanum* ["human race"]"), and goes on to ask: "Vnde negetûot er noh mit sinero *passione*. daz iz ímo sí liebsam?" ("Does he not ensure with his *passio* ["passion"] that they are beloved of him?").[3]

Notker is also a commentator, and his methods can again be demonstrated with a slightly longer passage from the Psalter, one of his best-known works. Only small contemporary fragments remain, but a twelfth-century full text from Einsiedeln survives, although with the untranslated Latin elements glossed in German. Three fragments are known from the same period, as is a Bavarian version from Wessobrunn, now known as the *Wiener Notker*. Other manuscripts are known to have existed, and a Bavarian text of the fourteenth century gives evidence of a continued survival.[4] Notker's method, here as in other German works, is simple. He presents the Latin text, sometimes with additions, and, in the case of metrical passages, sometimes rearrangements for the sake of clarity. The Latin is then translated, with additional comments. The German sometimes contains Latin elements left untranslated.

In his translations, then, Notker combines text and commentary. For the Psalter he uses (as he tells Hugo of Sion) an exposition by Augustine, but he also uses a wide range of others, which are sometimes difficult to identify.[5] The additions may be exegetical or etymological, and we often hear the teacher explaining individual words. The Psalter opens with the Latin text: "BEATVS VIR QVI NON ABIIT IN CONSILIO IM-PIORVM," which is translated freely but accurately: "DER. MÁN. IST. SÁLIG. der in dero argon rât negegieng" ("Blessed is the man who hath not walked in the counsel of the ungodly"). Still in German, Notker goes on to offer an example, taken from Augustine, but simplified, of a man who *did* take the wrong advice: "SO ADÂM téta. dô er déro chénun râtes fólgeta uuider Góte" ("as Adam did, when he took his wife's advice, and not God's"). Now comes the next part of the biblical verse in Latin: "Et in uia peccatorum non stetit" ("nor stood in the way of sinners"), again translated literally by Notker: "Noh an déro súndigon uuége nestûont." Notker is still referring to Adam, who "came to the broad road that leads to hell and stood upon it, because he followed his desires. In following, he stood." He is still using Augustine, but the allusion to Matthew 7:13 is found in other Psalm commentaries. The third clause of this first verse of the Psalter ("nor sat in the chair of pestilence") is translated, and then expounded in two ways. First, the Adam-parallel is continued. "Nor has sat on the throne of pestilence. I mean, he has not desired to rule, for that pestilence destroys in the end, as it did Adam, who wanted to become God." After this, however, Notker embarks upon an etymology, leaving in Latin the words *pestis* ("plague") and *pestilentia* ("pestilence"), the key words: "*Pestis* comes from *latine pecora sternens*. When *Pestis* spreads it is *pestilentia,* that is, *late peruagata pestis.*" Notker's source is not known. In the Einsiedeln codex, the two explanatory phrases are glossed *fiêo nider-slahinde* ("beast-destroying") and *uuíto uuâllonde stérbo* ("wide-ranging death").

In the Psalm manuscripts there are also found various catechetical texts, the Lord's Prayer, the Creed, and the Magnificat, as well as various other canticles—of Isaiah, Ezechias, Anna, Moses, and Habacuc. The treatment in all cases is the same as that of the Psalms.[6]

Reference has been made to the *Marriage of Philology and Mercury.* An eleventh-century manuscript from St. Gallen contains the first two of the nine books of *De Nuptiis,* with Notker's translation and commentary, which derives, in this case, from an exposition of the work by Remigius of Auxerre (ca. 841–908), who is named in a preface, with a number of other sources. Whether Notker translated any more of this very well known book is unclear.[7]

Notker's version of Boethius's *De Consolatione Philosophiae* is one of many versions of the *Consolation* made throughout and after the Middle Ages in Europe. In England, for example, the work was translated both by King

Aelfred the Great and by Queen Elizabeth I. Notker's version is known from one manuscript only, which is, like the Latin text from which he worked, still in St. Gallen. A prologue, which Notker also translates, tells us about the work, and how, in the sixth century, the statesman Boethius was put to death by his master Theoderic, the Dietrich of the *Hildebrandslied*. Boethius composed the *Consolation* under sentence of death, in the form of a dialogue between himself and the Lady Philosophy. Commentaries by Remigius and others in the Middle Ages placed emphasis on the Christian implications of the debate, and Notker once more uses several sources in expounding the work. The method is familiar. The passage which introduces Philosophy, for example, stresses the extraordinary power of her eyes, "burning and keen beyond the usual power of men," and Notker, having translated this, adds how the eyes of Philosophy may penetrate the depths of divine knowledge: "Ióh *profunda dei* gesíhet *philosophia*"—the crucial ideas being left in Latin.[8]

Notker's treatment of the Aristotelian works is similar, but in this case the question of source is rather more complex. At this time Aristotle was not, of course, known in Greek in medieval Germany, but five centuries earlier Boethius had planned to translate all the works of Aristotle into Latin. Even if it was to remain incomplete, Boethius's translations and commentaries are a considerable achievement. St. Gallen owned copies of two of the smaller works of Aristotle, the *Categories* and the *Hermeneutics*, and these were translated by Notker. In his preface to the latter he sums the works up. "Aristotiles scréib cathegorias. chúnt ze tûenne. uuáz éin lúzzíu uuórt pezéichenên. nû uuíle er sámo chúnt ketûon in perierminiis. uuáz zesámine gelégitíu bezéichenên" ("Aristotle wrote the *Categories* to make clear the meaning of individual words. Now in the *Hermeneutics* [Notker uses a variant Greek title] he turns to relationships").[9]

Notker does not provide a translation of Aristotle's work itself in either case. Boethius's translation of the *Categories*, in fact, appears in a St. Gallen manuscript followed by his own commentary, in which he repeated the text in an abridged form. Thus Notker had two versions of the text and a commentary before him, and he drew on other commentaries as well, using as before a mixture of German and Latin. For the *Hermeneutics* (known in Latin as *De Interpretatione*) Boethius wrote not one but two commentaries, for different levels of students, both of which include the text itself. In this case, then, Notker had three versions, and the identification of his sources for this work is very complicated indeed.

Notker's own Latin works include an *Art of Rhetoric*, known in three manuscripts, the work which includes the enigmatic German verses about the great boar referred to in an earlier chapter. One of the three manuscripts also contains another rhetorical work, *On Syllogisms,* in which Latin sentences are in fact followed by German translations. A fragmentary logic text found in a Viennese codex, and known either literally as *Bruchstücke einer Logik* or *De Definitione* [On Definition] (MSD LXXXI, St. XXV), seems to consist of extracts from Notker, as does a further work entitled *De Partibus Logicae* [The Branches of Logic], present in all three of the manuscripts containing the *Rhetoric,* that containing the *De Definitione,* and a further codex as well. This gives an indication of the popularity of the question-and-answer school text. For German studies, it is of interest as including the sequence of proverbial phrases in the vernacular, which demonstrate the concept of inevitability (MSD XXVII/1, St. LXXXVI, Lb. XXIII/18), and to which reference has again already been made. Notker's *Computus* is a table for reckoning the time of Easter, and it survives in two manuscripts.[10]

Finally, Notker's little work *On Music* is of special interest as the only one to be written—apart from technical terms—entirely in German. None of the five manuscripts is complete, but the surviving chapters deal with the production and nature of musical sound. Interest in music in monastic circles at this period was either practical, for liturgical singing, or philosophical, drawing conclusions from natural note relationships. Here again Notker makes use of Boethius, whose own work on music bridges the gap between Greek thought and the Middle Ages.[11]

Notker saw himself as an innovator in his use of German, and as a teacher he was respected: we can guess this from contemporary comment and from the dissemination of his works. His skill with the German language is undeniable, and his part in the creation of a philosophical and rhetorical vocabulary, while not easy to determine absolutely, is likely to have been extensive. He remains a teacher, however, and his use of German remains a functional one, designed for the better understanding of Latin theology. We have moved on from the glosses and the early translators, but have not yet reached a fully literary prose.

Williram

Notker's successor in the use of mixed German and Latin is Williram, abbot of the Bavarian monastery of Ebersberg from 1048 until his death in 1085. Of his major work, a commentary on the Song of Songs, written in about 1060, twenty-two manuscripts are known, some contemporary, others dating from as late as the sixteenth century, written just before the work first appeared in print. The commentary provided, furthermore, the basis for an interpretation of the Song of Songs written about a century later, the *St. Trudpert Song of Songs.*

Williram was a well-connected and ambitious cleric from a Rhineland Frankish family who studied at Fulda and was later in charge of the school attached to Bamberg cathedral, a cultural center of some significance. He was in personal contact with Henry III of Bavaria, and seems to have enjoyed some favor. In 1048, however, he became abbot of Ebersberg, away from the court, for reasons which are unclear. Any further ambitions were left unrealized. In addition to the work on the Canticles, Williram produced a Latin hagiographical work, some Latin verse, and his own epitaph.[12]

Williram is not, however, a German writer. It is misleading to consult the extracts printed in the *Lesebuch* (Lb. XXIV) and elsewhere, which give a German text of the Canticles commentary, perhaps with some Latin words in italics. The commentary is a far more complex work, conceived as a whole, and defeating all of the familiar generic classifications. To concentrate upon the German alone is to give that part a false emphasis.

The biblical book of Canticles, the Song of Songs, has been subjected to a variety of interpretative approaches. Later writers than Williram would take the lovers' dialogue that it contains as one between Christ and the soul, leading to the mystical union with the heavenly bridegroom. The St. Trudpert version points in this direction. Williram, though, takes it to be between the church, *ecclesia,* and Christ, and the whole is an allegory of the redemption. Thus for Canticles 1:2 (I, 3): "Thy name is as oil poured out; therefore young maidens have loved thee," the oil is seen as the name of Christ, spread far and wide to give the name "Christian," while the maidens are the souls, made young and clothed in garments of innocence by baptism.

Williram's work is tripartite, and most of the manuscripts reflect the original concept. It is arranged in three columns, the central column containing the biblical text. This is flanked on the left by Latin hexameters, which paraphrase and interpret the Bible, and on the right by a German translation of the hexameters, with a prose commentary in mixed German and Latin not unlike that used by Notker. An eleventh-century codex, now in Rome, uses the division as a basis for fine decoration, for example, separating the columns by walls and arches, echoing church architecture. Other manuscripts also have headings to indicate which voice is speaking at any point—*vox ecclesiae, vox Christi* ("the voice of the church," "the voice of Christ").

Williram tells us about his design in a Latin preface: the composed portions encircle the Bible text, which is, at the same time, in the most important position. The German section is intended as an aid to the understanding of the Latin verses. There is an older tradition of providing simpler Latin prose versions of difficult metrical texts, but Williram uses instead a mixed language. In pedagogical terms the German might be used either to help with the reading of the Latin or as a lead-in toward it or indeed as a commentary in its own right. Both outside columns serve to explain the central text, however.

The preface tells us a little about the sources. Williram does not claim, and indeed denies, originality: he has added "nothing of his own," but has made his commentary from the writings of the Fathers. In fact his main source is a Canticles commentary by Haimo, bishop of Auxerre in the ninth century, together with some other commentaries. To take once again a brief extract in illustration of the work, Canticles 2:3 stands at the center: "As the apple tree among the trees of the woods, so is my beloved among the sons. I sat down under his shadow, whom I desired; and his fruit was sweet unto my palate." *Ecclesia* is speaking. Williram divides the verse, and for the latter part of it offers in the left-hand column four hexameters in explanation: "He provides me now with sweet shade against the sun, / and lets me take the ripe fruit, / he whose right hand protects me in adversity, / and who will fulfill me with his countenance forever." The German text both simplifies and expands this, translating the first two lines, but going on to say that "I have his protection *in persecutionibus* ("when persecuted") and *in feruore temptationis* ("in the heat of temptation")." Christ, too, will fulfill his *ecclesia* in *contemplationem suae divinitatis* ("the contemplation of his divinity").

The use of German is comparable with that of Notker (and, indeed, Williram also uses the system of accents). With Williram, however, the Latin elements, usually direct quotations from the commentaries of Haimo and others, fall at the end of clauses, giving a more regular balance. As Hans Eggers has pointed out, Williram's German sentences "almost always build up toward a conclusion which is Latin, on which lies the whole weight of the expression; the keystone is missing from the artistic German arch."[13] This is the case in the passage cited above: when Williram is rendering what is in fact contained in the Bible verse, he writes in German. The commentary moves toward Latin conclusions, though, from the protection *in persecutionibus,* to the ultimate *contemplationem suae diuinitatis.*

Williram's German vocabulary includes words which are not found in earlier texts, but he also uses a number of others that are found only in writings which predate Notker. Whether he is deliberately using words which were genuinely old-fashioned is a matter of debate, however, just as we do not know whether the unattested words are his own.

The work is a complex one, difficult for a modern reader to classify, and the transition to print damages the work considerably. Williram's commentary on the Canticles was designed in three manuscript columns, and this formal aspect is as important as the content. The three sections are interdependent, and the German element is relatively small. That it is present at all, however, is of some significance.

The Influence of Notker

A group of smaller Old High German prose pieces may be linked, albeit fairly tenuously, with Notker. An eleventh-century codex from St. Gallen contains a series of sample letters, among them a text which used to be known as "Ruodpert's Letter," although it is now more properly termed *St. Galler Schularbeit* [St. Gallen School Exercise] (MSD LXXX, St. XXVI, Lb. XXIII/19). It consists of a group of Latin words and phrases, some deriving from Notker, with German translations. The words include the names of the parts of speech in German.

Other smaller prose writings are linked with the so-called *Wiener Notker* [Vienna Notker], the eleventh-century Bavarian adaptation of the Psalter made probably at Wessobrunn, and containing only Psalms 1–50 and 101–150.[14] The adaptor has pared down Notker's text, leaving intact only the strictly theological parts of the commentary. The original manuscript has been cut up, and some of the additional works originally contained in it have turned up in the bindings of early printed books. One such fragment is the *Geistliche Ratschläge* [Spiritual Advice] (MSD LXXXV, St. XXXI), which consists of a list of biblical characters who are to be emulated. "If you would be obedient, take the example of Abraham . . . ," and so on. The source is a commentary by Gregory the Great on Ezechiel, although the composer of the German text probably worked from a set of extracts rather than from the original.

Similar in terms of survival is a group of sermons, some fragments of which remain in the Vienna-Wessobrunn codex, while others have been rescued from bindings. The major anthologies divide the *Wessobrunn Sermons* (MSD LXXXVI, St. XXX, XXXII–XXXIII, Lb. XXVII) into three sections. The first section, with parts of three sermons, derives from the works of Augustine, and the second, four sermons still in the original codex, from the Gospel homilies of Gregory the Great, sometimes quite closely translated. The final and very fragmentary group contains versions of sermons by Bede, as well as an adaptation from the Benedictine Rule.

The long catechetical text known as the *Third Wessobrunn Confession*, an adaptation for women, found in the Vienna Notker codex, has been discussed in an earlier chapter. The original of this adaptation, it will be recalled, is a version from Bamberg, and the Bamberg Confession is followed in the manuscript by a work known as *Himmel und Hölle* [Heaven and Hell] (MSD XXX, St. XXIX). It is possible that the work was also present in the Vienna Notker manuscript, but has been lost. This piece is in so rhythmic a prose that it has been thought of as a kind of poem. Its description of heaven and hell takes the form of two lists, of virtues and then of sins, the latter expressed negatively, as the lack of specific virtues. In terms of language the work is powerful, and its extended vision of heaven and hell is comparable to those found in the *Muspilli* and by Otfrid. The source is not known, but the material is commonplace, deriving from the Apocalypse and elsewhere. Heaven "nebedarf des sunnen noh des manskimen da ze liehtenne" ("needs no light from sun or moon to light it"), and hell is "beches gerouche, der sterkiste sveuelstank, uerwazzenlich genibile, des tódes scategruoba . . ." ("smoke of pitch, the strongest stink of sulfur, mists of abomination and the shadowy grave"). The genre and purpose of the work are unclear, and it has some affinities with the sermon, but the link with the Confession, which precedes it in the Bamberg manuscript, remains strong.[15]

Otloh's Prayer and the Prayer from Klosterneuburg

Two prose prayers are known from the end of the Old High German period. The first of these is known as the *Klosterneuburg Prayer* (MSD LXXXIV, St. XXXIV), from its provenance in the Austrian monastery of that name. It is in the Bavarian dialect, and asks God to preserve man from sin, since he is created in God's image and redeemed by Christ's blood. It asks for forgiveness for past, present, and future sins, now and at the hour of death. Like the earlier *Frankish Prayer,* the piece is liturgical in tone.

Rather more interesting is another Bavarian prayer of the eleventh century, this time by a relatively well-known writer. Otloh of St. Emmeram was born at the beginning of that century, and took monastic vows (after some hesitation) in 1032 at St. Emmeram, the Regensburg monastery with a considerable literary tradition. In the course of his life—he died about 1070—Otloh moved about between St. Emmeram and the monasteries of Fulda and of Amorbach in the Odenwald, but he was very much bound up with St. Emmeram, and he died there. He was extremely prolific as a writer and as a copyist, although he was by no means as committed to German as Otfrid, Notker, or even Williram. Most of his works are in Latin and are either hagiographical or penitential, although he also wrote an interesting, if stylized, autobiography (which tells us, for example, how the devil tried to keep him from the right path by making him unable to get up in the morning in time for matins). Otloh also composed a prose prayer in Latin which was copied several times. There is also a metrical Latin version of it, but more important in the present context is the existence of a German translation, *Otlohs Gebet* [Otloh's Prayer] (MSD LXXXIII, St. XXXV, Lb. XXVI), appearing in a manuscript originally from St. Emmeram, which was either written or corrected by Otloh himself, and it follows a Latin version. The German version has the rubric "German prayer, from the above," but the relationship is, unfortunately, not so simple. The German version is shorter, and several apparently important passages are omitted. Rather earlier in the same codex, however, we have yet another Latin version of the prayer which is closer to the German. Otloh seems, in fact, to have varied the text considerably, and it is impossible to say which is the "final" version.[16]

The German text first asks God for personal protection against sin, for true belief, and for virtue. The second part is a litany invoking the protection of a number of saints, and the last part calls for God's mercy for Otloh's monastery "destroyed through our sinfulness"—St. Emmeram had undergone a variety of troubles in the 1050s and was burned in 1062. The prayer will have been written rather later. The prayer also asks mercy for the town and for the monastic community, although not (as in the Latin text) for the Pope and the emperor.

The German seems less polished than the Latin. There is a marked repetition of the phrase *Dara nah* ("And then"), which is not present in the original, and the German sometimes ends (as does Williram's prose) in Latin, especially in the litany section. It is unclear whether or not this is deliberate. The prayer is not particularly important within the framework of Otloh's writings as a whole, but that it should occur to him at all to put the prayer into the vernacular is interesting. It is, though, perhaps just another variation upon a work of which he seems to have been fond.

Chapter Twelve
Development and Expansion

A language changes slowly, and written language tends in any case to be conservative, so that it is well-nigh impossible to determine when a language-period ends. Two major sound-changes distinguish between Old High German and its following stage, Middle High German: the spread of the vowel modification known as *Umlaut,* and the weakening to a neutral sound (usually shown as *e*), or indeed the complete loss, of unstressed full vowels. This is of course an oversimplification, but the changes (which are not simultaneous), are distinctive. Thus Old High German *furi* ("for") undergoes modification of its main vowel, which is caused by the next vowel, the *i*; since that is unstressed, it is lost, and we arrive at the familiar form *für.* The weakening is clear in words which appear in the Tatian translation, say, as *fólgeta* ("followed") and *giségenot* ("blessed"), and later as *folgte* and *gesegnet.* These changes begin to be visible in writing in the early to mid-eleventh century, and are pretty well complete at the end of the twelfth, the period between, say, 1050 and 1170 being one of transition. Language studies have linked this time of transition with the later linguistic phase and refer to it as early Middle High German. It has also come to be seen as a quite distinct literary period. For all that, all the major anthologies of Old High German—even that of Steinmeyer, who claims to have omitted Middle High German texts—contain at least some later works with the linguistic features of early Middle High German.

Gustav Ehrismann insisted on the separate nature of German writings in the transitional period by devoting an entire volume of his literary history to them. His opening statement expresses views which persisted for a long time. "The German poetry that has its rebirth around the middle of the eleventh century depends on an entirely new set of conditions. A new piety had arisen, in which the gulf between God and the world was the absolute and dominant thought."[1] For Ehrismann there had been a gap in the development of German literature, and a fresh start marked by a religious intensity which he associated with a set of reforms in

Benedictine monasticism originated in the monastery of Cluny in France in the tenth century.

All this begs a number of questions. Notker, Otloh, and Williram provide a continuity in the eleventh century. If the gap applies to poetry in its strictest sense, there is indeed nothing comparable with Otfrid until the eleventh century. But Old High German survivals are few in any case, and there were some post-Otfridian poems, at least, on a variety of themes, composed in the tenth century. Indeed, most of the Old High German we possess was written down precisely during the supposed gap, and this too is not insignificant.

The link with Cluny is no longer accepted. The reform movement was limited in Germany, and was in any case monastic, while not all the works of the transitional period are from monastic sources. This itself, it is true, may be seen as a novelty, but the ideas expressed in the poems are not new. What Ehrismann took for a new piety is often a more skilled expression of familiar theological ideas. There is no general stress on asceticism, and other attempts to find some kind of unity have failed.[2]

Certainly there is an increase in the number of surviving works. The bulk of writing is still theological, however, so that German remains in essence a means for the dissemination of ideas, rather than a literary medium for its own sake, something which it does not become until the Middle High German period proper. Whether we may speak of a genuine continuity between the Old High German and the later writers is questionable. Otfrid and Notker both saw themselves as innovators, and all the Old High German works are in some respects isolated. But the small tributaries are beginning to flow and to grow together, and there is certainly a thematic continuity between the earliest works and those of the transitional period. Major developments taking place in Latin theology in the eleventh century do not affect German writing for some time, and the theology remains conservative. Nor is it even particularly ascetic. The stress on the need to strive toward salvation might imply a rejection of the world, but what remains in the foreground is the *possibility* of that salvation, and the exegetical imagery remains largely the same.

There are, of course, some superficial differences. The smaller Old High German works owe their survival largely to chance, and the earliest of the transitional period texts are also preserved incomplete at the end of manuscripts. Soon, however, we encounter collective codices, manuscripts devoted to German theological writings, anthologies which sometimes just copy, sometimes update considerable numbers of texts. Changes are evident, too, in author and audience. The literary centers were initially the monasteries, but already in the eleventh century we begin to see the hand of the secular clergy—priests attached to courts, cathedrals, or cathedral schools (Bamberg and Regensburg are examples). More types of writing are now attested, even if the new basic material is treated in the same fashion as earlier works. There are some improvements in technique, and in this context we may speak of a real continuity. Rhyme was not, of course, reinvented, but it was polished, and more regular metrical and strophic forms appear. There has been much debate on the change from Otfrid's long-line to a genuine couplet, and the manuscripts do not help us. Modern printed texts are inconsistent in their presentation, too. There are arguments, at least, for the continuity of the Otfridian line as a basic formal unit at least until the beginning of the twelfth century.[3]

Some works of the transitional period have already been examined—Williram, for example. In that context, we saw how his work was continued in the *St. Trudpert Song of Songs,* and there are other later prose translations of Latin theological texts, including one by Alcuin on the virtues, and a medieval compendium of theology plus general knowledge known as the *Lucidarius.* In the discussion of the glosses we were able to look ahead to the *Summarium Heinrici* and beyond; and the charms, too, persist right through to modern times. With the charms, indeed, there is plainly a continuity in the real sense. The transitional period does, it is true, provide us with a greater number of medical-scientific texts, lapidaries, herbaria, and recipe-books proper, but we may recall here the *Innsbruck Pharmacopoeia,* which consists largely of simples. But under the rubric "to stop nosebleeds" comes first a Latin charm, and then a practical recipe in a mixture of Latin and German.[4]

Sermons, too, serve as a bridge between Old High German and the later periods. In the second group of sermon fragments from Wessobrunn (MSD LXXXVIb, St. XXXII/4), for example, there is a comment on the healing of the blind man at Jericho (Luke 18:35–43) linking him with man in general, "driven blind from paradise into exile here . . . until his eyes were opened by the son of God." The fruit of the tree in Eden has opened Adam's eyes in one sense (Genesis 3:7) but made him, and his progeny, blind to God until the redemption. The notion—which we saw in Otfrid—of man as the exile, returning to his homeland is also found in a collection of sermons known as the *Speculum Ecclesiae* [Mirror of the Church] from Benediktbeuern. In the context of Psalm 136:4, "How shall we sing the song of the Lord in a strange land?" the sermon explains that "we are in exile from God . . . and should weep and strive daily to be able to return to our homeland."[5] Sermons are the one part of the divine service regularly in the vernacular, and their tone is felt in many of the poetic works from the transitional period, although the term "rhymed sermon" is probably better avoided, since the use was not the same.

A few works only must serve to demonstrate the continuity of ideas in the period. Closest to the *Evangelienbuch* is a poem written in the late eleventh century known as the *Altdeutsche* or *Wiener Genesis* [Early German or Vienna Genesis]. The work mixes narrative and commentary in over three thousand long-lines, with some stress on the tropological sense. Otfrid, telling us of the redemption, refers often to the fall, and this poem now treats in full the opposite pole of the divine plan of history. Adam and Eve are driven from Paradise into exile, and demand our pity, although they are also an example. We shall not return to Paradise until we give up sin. Even so, the poet points onward within his narrative. The redeemer will come, and then "Adam's fall will be wiped out by the death of God, who is without sin. Thus we may sing *laus tibi domine.*" This praise to God is the center of the poem's theme.[6] The narrative parts are, however, generally more expansive than Otfrid's, and there is, for example, an extended Joseph story which is found again in a collective codex from the monastery of Vorau in Austria, which also contains a rather different poem on Genesis, although the ideas are similar once again. Adam and Eve go into exile "into Babylon, where everything is dark and blind."[7] The Vienna Genesis itself was revised later in the period and there are other biblical narratives—the genre continues into Middle High German and later.

More lyrical expressions of the same ideas are found in an early and impressive work known as *Ezzos Gesang* [Ezzo's Song], which is known in two forms (MSD XXXI, Lb. XLIII). The older of the two is a fragment of seven strophes, each with six or eight long-lines. The later is a full text in the Vorau codex. From the later version and from Latin sources we know that the work was written at the instigation of Bishop Gunther of Bamberg in about 1060 by Ezzo, with a (lost) tune by Wille. The Vorau text has thirty-four strophes, mirroring the years of Christ's life, and the theology, too, is familiar. What is new is a controlled conciseness. The sixth strophe of the fragmentary version (in a manuscript from Ochsenhausen in Swabia) puts forward a complete *summa theologiae,* telling how all was dark when Adam fell, with only a few stars, obscured and giving little light, for they were overshadowed by *diu nebiluinster naht* ("the misty gloom of night") which comes from the devil. But the devil's power is past, and there now appears (or "shines": the verb is *erskein*) the son of God, who is a true sun (the word puns in German) in the heavens.[8]

With the Vorau version it is unclear how much is original. Comparison with the strophes of the earlier version shows that the work has been expanded, but scholars have not agreed on which of the later ones are new. Heinz Rupp, for example, sees one original strophe in strophes 27, 28, and 29 of the Vorau text, and rejects what he sees as added explanatory comments.[9] In strophe 27, however, the poet tells the story of the Paschal Lamb and the marking of the doors by the Israelites to avert the angel of death (Exodus 12), going on to say that "that was all spiritual, and signifies Christian facts," just as Otfrid does, for example, when explaining the gifts of the Magi. Strophe 28 has a concise imagery which cannot be thought of as teaching, but only as reinforcing ideas familiar to the audience. This, too, sometimes happens with the *Evangelienbuch,* of course. "The Paschal Lamb," the poet tells us, "lay on the altar of the cross . . . and laid waste the lands of the old tyrant. The devil and his army were swallowed in the red baptismal sea." The strophe links the two Testaments, and the compound *daz rote tovfmere* ("red baptismal sea") links the Red Sea, which drowned Pharaoh, with baptism and with Christ's blood as defeating the devil. The following strophe, incidentally, tells us how Christ gives us a free return to our homeland (*erbelant*)—the paradisiacal homeland once more.

The Ochsenhausen manuscript contains another German poem which has been given the title *Memento mori* [Think on Death], which is again strophic, having nineteen groups of four long-lines. A passage is missing in the middle, however, and the scribe has joined two originally unconnected half-lines. It is unlikely that much is missing (MSD XXXb, Lb. XLII). The opening of the poem is homiletic, addressing an audience of "men and women," and the world is contrasted with Paradise. Here the stress is on the need for right behavior in a world that can corrupt. The corrupt middle portion contains a discussion on the concept of "right" and the purchase of legal justice, and these lines have been seen as a reference to contemporary historical circumstances. The stress of equality within the law and the possibility of malpractice recalls the admonitions of the *Muspilli,* a poem similar in many respects, although perhaps intended for a more restricted audience. There is a strong sense of human unity in this later work, in the common descent from Adam, and the central theological points of the poem are again familiar. The idea of the world as a deceiver is brought out again at the end of the work, but man has free choice and can make the right decision. The poem ends with a prayer that God may grant us—again the tone of the sermon—the power to do so. Right at the end of the poem, however, is the comment "fro so muozint ir wesin iemer:

daz machot all ein noker," meaning: "may you ever be happy. That was by Noker." The slightly incongruous line looks like the closing benediction of a sermon. The identity of the author as Noker (or Nogger) of Zwiefalten, who died in 1095 and had some connections with the monastic reforms, has been claimed, but this remains unclear. The point is of small literary importance.[10]

New forms arise in religious poetry, new vehicles for the continued theology. Old High German rhymed prayers are brief, but the transitional period produces lengthy penitential poems, *Sündenklagen,* and then, rather later, hymns to the Virgin, which also exploit biblical exegesis in a concise fashion. The saints' lives of the early period have later parallels in individual works and in the massive *Kaiserchronik* [Chronicle of the Emperors], with over seventeen thousand lines in rhymed couplets. It is included in the Vorau codex and there are other manuscripts. The *Georgslied* itself is recalled in works like the rhymed *Life of John the Baptist* from Baumgartenberg on the Danube, an early twelfth-century poem which tells how the Baptist "commanded the dead to rise up, gave light to the blind . . . opened the ears of the deaf," and so on. There are several poems on the Baptist, in fact, one of them by the first named woman writer in German, Frau Ava, who composed other biblical and hagiographical poems.[11]

A more contemporary saint is depicted in the *Annolied* [Song of Anno]. Anno was archbishop of Cologne until his death in 1075, and was officially proclaimed a saint in 1183. The poem (the manuscript of which is lost) was probably written not long after his death, and it covers in forty-eight strophes the creation of the world, Old Testament and later history, and then the life of Anno, stressing, for example, his good works among the poor and the sick.[12]

With the *Annolied* we come close to a new development in the transitional language period: the handling of secular themes within a religious framework. Thus a priest called Lamprecht adapted a French version of the adventures of Alexander the Great, laying great emphasis on the moral point of the vanity of all worldly gains. A little later, in the mid-twelfth century, a Bavarian priest called Konrad translated (he tells us) from French into Latin and then into German a long poem on the fall of the hero Roland at the battle of Roncesvalles, against the Saracens in 778. Konrad gives us plenty of vivid battlescenes, but the bias is still theological. Where other versions depict Roland as a Christian, but somewhat arrogant, warrior-hero (as in the *Chanson de Roland,* the Old French *Song of Roland,* which predates Konrad, although it was not his direct source), he is seen here far more strongly as a martyr, leaving the outcome of the battle to God's disposition of events. Konrad's work, though, is still of epic length and breadth.[13]

During the early Middle High German language period, there must have been a continuation of the secular tradition in literature, but we can again only speculate on lost works. It is likely that there were heroic poems that would lead later to the Middle High German *Nibelungenlied* or the Dietrich epics, in which the name of Hildebrand is found again. To the twelfth century, too, belong the earliest written examples of a genuinely secular literature in the precourtly epic of *Rother,* and the adventure-story *Herzog Ernst* [Duke Ernst]. These are, however, from the last years of the transition period.

Two final works do, however, merit consideration. Both are from the eleventh century, and both are included in the Old High German anthologies. The first was named *Merigarto* [The World] by its first editor, and the manuscript is very difficult to read. *Merigarto* (MSD XXXII, Lb. XLI) consists of about 120 long-lines, separated by rubrics, and concerned largely with seas and rivers, telling how they were created by God and endowed with magical properties, such as the ability to heal (or cause) blindness, change color, cure infertility, and so on. Five central strophes, under a rubric "On Bishop Reginbert," tells how the poet fled from a dispute "between two bishops" (hence probably during the ecclesiastical conflicts with the state in the eleventh century) to Utrecht, where he met a certain Reginbert, who had visited Iceland, and who tells him about that far-off place, where the ice, as hard as crystal, "can be heated, so that it glows, and men can heat their rooms and cook with it." Reginbert may not have been a bishop—perhaps the rubricator was misled by the reference to the two bishops earlier—and in any event he is unidentified. But the emergence of this kind of geographical gnomic poem, rhymed information glorifying God's creation, but concentrating on particularly interesting aspects of it, is of some interest.[14]

Comparable, but with a far more diversified tradition, is the so-called *Physiologus,* which combines theology with zoology. It originates in Greece in the early centuries of the Christian era, as a collection of animal descriptions, and later on, theological interpretations of the animals were added. Medieval Latin versions abound, and the work is known in most European vernaculars. In German, a prose version dates from about 1070 (MSD LXXXII, St. XXVII, Lb. XXV extracts), and another, slightly later version is found in the same manuscript as the *Vienna Genesis.* This in its turn was adapted into verse, and the tradition continues to the

Reformation. The number of animals described varies. There is nothing to link the work with the reform movements, and the theological method is traditional. To take a familiar example, we are told of the unicorn that it may be captured when it lays its head in the lap of a virgin. This is seen as an allegory of the Virgin Birth, and the nature of the beast as a goatlike creature (the similarity to a horse occurs later) is linked with Christ's adoption of sinful flesh. Not all the beasts are mythical, of course, and the interest must certainly have been in the zoology, practical or fanciful, as much as in the theology. Nevertheless, the theology is present. For the modern reader, incidentally, it is well to recall how improbable an elephant might seem, had one not seen one, and how eminently plausible a unicorn.[15]

The early Middle High German period—to retain the linguistic term—shows, then, an expansion of interests in works like the *Physiologus,* a broadening in the themes for which the German language is used, but on a continued base of traditional biblical interpretation. So too there is a tightening of poetic skills in works like *Ezzos Gesang,* and the development of a wider range of types of poetry. Most of the literature remains linked with the bulk of Old High German writings—completely secular texts remain isolated. But the German language has gained a range of literary experience within a functional theological framework.

We may conclude with a farewell verse of the kind regularly found at the close of manuscripts. Even taken out of its context at the end of a list of nuns, the German and Latin *Bilsener Schlußvers* [Verse from Bilsen (near Maastricht] (MSD L) is appropriate.

> Tesi samanunga   vvas edele unde scôna
> Et omnium uirtutum   pleniter plena.
>
> (This collection was fine and noble,
> And very full of all the virtues.)

Notes and References

Chapter One

1. See W. Schröder, "Grenzen und Möglichkeiten einer althochdeutschen Literaturgeschichte," *Berichte . . . der sächsischen Akademie* (Leipzig), phil.-hist. Kl. 105/ii (1959), and W. Mohr and W. Haug, *Zweimal Muspilli* (Tübingen, 1977), p. 71.

2. W. Braune, *Althochdeutsche Grammatik,* cited from the 5th ed. (1935), §6a; see 13th ed. by H. Eggers (Tübingen, 1975),§4. See also H. Eggers, *Deutsche Sprachgeschichte I. Das Althochdeutsche* (Reinbek bei Hamburg, 1963).

3. C. McEvedy, *Penguin Atlas of Medieval History* (Harmondsworth: Penguin, 1961), offers a graphic survey. See too J. M. Wallace-Hadrill, *The Barbarian West,* 3d ed. (London: Hutchinson, 1967).

4. Wallace-Hadrill, *Barbarian West,* pp. 64–114, and P. Lasko, *The Kingdom of the Franks* (London: Thames and Hudson, 1971).

5. McEvedy, *Atlas,* p. 46.

6. R. Schützeichel, *Die Grundlagen des westlichen Mitteldeutschen* (Tübingen: Niemeyer, 1961), and "Neue Funde zur Lautverschiebung im Mittelfränkischen," *ZfdA* 93 (1964):19–30.

7. W. Sanders, "Die Buchstaben des Königs Chilperic," *ZfdA* 101 (1972):54–84.

8. B. Schreyer-Mühlpfordt, "Sprachliche Einigungstendenzen im deutschen Schrifttum des Frühmittelalters," *Wissenschaftliche Annalen* 5 (1956):295–304. See also H. Rupp, *Forschung zur althochdeutschen Literatur 1945–1962* (Stuttgart, 1965), p. 26f.

9. K. Matzel, "Das Problem der 'karlingischen Hofsprache,'" in: *Medievalia Litteraria. Festschrift für H. de Boor* (Munich, 1971), pp. 15–31.

10. H. D. Schlosser, *Die literarischen Anfänge der deutschen Sprache* (Berlin, 1977), has a clear survey, p. 37f.

11. E. Sievers, *Deutsche Sagversdichtung* (Heidelberg: Winter, 1924); R. Koegel, *Geschichte der deutschen Literatur* (Strasbourg: Trübner, 1894–97). See J. S. Groseclose and B. Murdoch, *Die althochdeutschen poetischen Denkmäler* (Stuttgart, 1976), pp. 1–30.

12. A good general survey is that by K. C. King, *The Earliest German Monasteries* (Nottingham, 1961).

13. Studies include J. M. Clark, *The Abbey of St. Gall* (Cambridge: Cambridge University Press, 1926); S. Sonderegger, *Althochdeutsch in St. Gallen* (St. Gallen, 1970); G. Baesecke, "Das althochdeutsche Schrifttum von Reichenau," *PBB* 51 (1927):206–22; B. Bischoff, "Literarisches und künstlerisches Leben in St. Emmeram," in his *Mittelalterliche Studien* (Stuttgart: Hiersemann, 1966–67), 2:77–115; B. Bischoff, *Lorsch im Spiegel seiner Handschriften* (Munich: Arbeo-Gesellschaft, 1974); I. Schröbler, "Fulda und die althochdeutsche Literatur," *Jahrbuch der Görres-Gesellschaft* 1 (1960):1–26. See too R. Sullivan, "The Carolingian Missionary and the Pagans," *Speculum* 28 (1953):705–40.

14. The text is in H. D. Schlosser, *Althochdeutsche Literatur* (Frankfurt/M. and Hamburg, 1970), p. 254f. See H. Mettke's comparable anthology, *Älteste deutsche Dichtung und Prosa* (Leipzig, 1976), pp. 84–87. The most readily available collections of facsimiles are those by G. Eis, *Altdeutsche Handschriften* (Munich, 1949), and H. Fischer, *Schrifttafeln zum althochdeutschen Lesebuch* (Tübingen, 1966). Of importance, too, is the general palaeographical study by B. Bischoff, "Paläographische Fragen deutscher Denkmäler der Karolingerzeit," *Frühmittelalterliche Studien* 5 (1971):104–34.

15. H. F. Massmann, *Gedrängtes althochdeutsches Wörterbuch* (Berlin, 1846), p. 43.

Chapter Two

1. The fullest recent study with texts is that by S. Opitz, *Südgermanische Runeninschriften* (Kirchzarten, 1977).

2. Eis, *Handschriften*, p. 32f. with facsimile.

3. See H. Tiefenbach, "Zur Binger Inschrift," *RVjb* 41 (1977):124–37, with photographs.

4. Wallace-Hadrill, *Barbarian West*, pp. 54–57 and 73f., has a concise survey. On the vocabulary, the best survey remains that by G. Baesecke, "Die deutschen Worte der germanischen Gesetze," *PBB* 59 (1935):1–101. There are translated extracts in Mettke, *Älteste Dichtung*, pp. 108–11.

5. Mettke, *Älteste Dichtung*, has a photograph, p. 48.

6. H. Tiefenbach, "Ein übersehener Textzeuge des Trierer Capitulare," *RVjb* 39 (1975):272–310.

7. See G. Ehrismann, *Geschichte der deutschen Literatur . . . I. Das Althochdeutsche,* 2d ed. (Munich, 1932), pp. 290–95.

8. Of the many language studies relevant here, see Eggers, *Das Althochdeutsche,* and two earlier studies: R. v. Raumer, *Die Einwirkung des Christentums auf die althochdeutsche Sprache,* published in Berlin in 1851 but now reprinted (Walluf bei Wiesbaden: Sändig, 1972), and T. Frings, *Grundlegung einer Geschichte der deutschen Sprache,* 3d ed. (Halle: Niemeyer, 1957), pp. 58–75.

9. *Forschung,* p. 28.

10. There is a good study of various translations by A. Masser, "Die althochdeutschen Übersetzungen des Vaterunsers," *PBB* (Tübingen) 85 (1963):35–45.

11. W. Betz, "Zum St Galler Paternoster," *PBB* (Halle) 82 (1961: Festschrift E. Karg-Gasterstädt):153–56, and more recently G. Must, "Das St Galler Paternoster," in: *Akten des V. Kongresses der IVG* (Berne and Frankfurt/M.: Lang, 1976), 2:396–403, try to justify the readings of the text, neither convincingly.

12. See G. Baesecke, "Die altdeutschen Beichten," *PBB* 49 (1925):268–355, and H. Eggers, "Die altdeutschen Beichten," *PBB* (Halle) 77 (1955):89–123; 80 (1958):372–403; and 81 (1959):78–122.

13. W. Vondrák, "Althochdeutsches in den slavischen Freisinger Denkmälern," *PBB* 22 (1897):201–8.

14. There is a fragmentary prayer (MSD vol. II, 42; St. LXXXIV) which may be that for the elevation of the chalice, but very little can be made of it. The Erfurt oath for Jews (MSD C) and the Swabian betrothal formula (MSD XCIX) are interesting, but fall outside the Old High German period.

Chapter Three

1. The best impression of the glosses is to be gained from the manuscripts. See G. Baesecke, *Lichtdrucke nach althochdeutschen Handschriften* (Halle, 1926) and his *Der deutsche Abrogans und die Herkunft des deutschen Schrifttums* (Halle, 1930).

2. See J. K. Bostock, *A Handbook on Old High German Literature*, 2d ed. by K. C. King and D. R. McLintock (Oxford, 1976), p. 91.

3. There is an example in J. Splett, "Zwei althochdeutsche Griffelglossen," *PBB* (Halle) 94 (1974):77–79.

4. See Baesecke, *Abrogans*. For full studies of the range of glosses, see R. Bergmann, *Verzeichnis der althochdeutschen und altsächsischen Glossenhandschriften* (Berlin and New York, 1973); H. Mayer, *Althochdeutsche Glossen: Nachtrag* (Toronto and Buffalo, 1974). Important recent studies include R. Bergmann, *Mittelfränkische Glossen* (Bonn: Röhrscheid, 1966). An *Althochdeutsches Glossenwörterbuch* is in progress, ed. T. Starck and J. C. Wells (Heidelberg, 1972ff.).

5. See H. Götz, "Kontextübersetzung und Vokabelübersetzung in althochdeutschen Glossen," *PBB* (Halle) 82 (1961: Festschrift E. Karg-Gasterstädt):139–52, and A. Schwarz, "Glossen als Text," *PBB* (Tübingen) 99 (1977):25–36.

6. H. v. Gadow, *Die althochdeutschen Aratorglossen* (Munich, 1974), chosen simply for convenience, to illustrate the gloss as such. The passages cited are on pp. 44, 51, 54, and 68.

7. Facsimile ed. B. Bischoff, J. Duft, and S. Sonderegger, *Das älteste deutsche Buch* (St. Gallen, 1977), and partial edition by G. Baesecke, *Der deutsche*

Abrogans (Halle, 1931). See W. Betz, *Der Einfluß des Lateinischen* . . . I. *Der Abrogans* (Heidelberg: Winter, 1936), and the major study by J. Splett, *Abrogans-Studien* (Wiesbaden, 1976).

8. J. Splett, *Samanunga-Studien* (Göppingen, 1979).

9. See G. Baesecke, *Der Vocabularius Sci Galli in der angelsächsischen Mission* (Halle: Niemeyer, 1933).

10. There is an abridged text in Ahd. G1. III, 58–349 and V, 33–37, but the work is cited here from *Summarium Heinrici,* ed. R. Hildebrandt (Berlin and New York, 1974ff.), 1:175. On the dating see in addition to Hildebrandt, W. Wegstein, "Anmerkungen zu *Summarium Heinrici,* " *ZfdA* 101 (1972):303–15, and (placing the work later) H. Wagner, "Zur Datierung des *Summarium Heinrici,*" *ZfdA* 104 (1975):118–26.

11. See for example R. Reiche, *Ein rheinisches Schulbuch aus dem 11. Jahrhundert* (Munich: Arbeo-Gesellschaft, 1976).

12. See for example such brief papers as that by H. Tiefenbach, "Althochdeutsche Bibelglossen aus Ellwangen," *ZfdA* 104 (1975):12–20.

13. F. Jolles, "The Hazards of Travel in Medieval Germany," *German Life and Letters* 21 (1967/8):309–19. See J. A. Huisman "Die Pariser Gespräche," *RVjb* 33 (1969):272–96, and W. Haubrichs, "Zur Herkunft der altdeutschen (Pariser) Gespräche," *ZfdA* 101 (1972):86–103.

14. See S. Sonderegger, "Frühe Übersetzungsschichten im Althochdeutschen," in: *Festschrift W. Henzen* (Berne, 1965), pp. 101–14.

15. Full text ed. U. Daab, *Die althochdeutsche Benediktinerregel* (Tübingen, 1959). See her *Studien zur* . . . *Benediktinerregel* (Halle, 1929), and also W. Betz, "Die Heimat der . . . Benediktinerregel," *PBB* 65 (1942):182–85.

16. W. Betz, *Deutsch und Lateinisch* (Bonn: Bouvier, 1949), is the major study of the language, with H. Ibach, "Zu Wortschatz und Begriffswelt der althochdeutschen Benediktinerregel," *PBB* (Halle) 78 (1956):1–110; 79 (1957):106–85; 80 (1958):190–271; 81 (1959):123–73; and 82 (1961/2):371–473.

17. Text in U. Daab, *Drei Reichenauer Denkmäler* (Tübingen, 1963), and in St. XXXVIII. See U. Daab, "Zur Datierung der altalemannischen Psalmenübersetzung," *PBB* (Tübingen) 83 (1961/2):281–301.

18. Texts in M. Heyne, *Kleinere altniederdeutsche Denkmäler* (Paderborn, 1877).

19. The major edition by E. Sievers, *Die Murbacher Hymnen* of 1874, has been reprinted with a useful introduction of E. S. Firchow (New York and London, 1972). See also Daab, *Denkmäler,* pp. 29–72, for a text.

20. The edition cited (by paragraph) is that by E. Sievers, *Tatian,* 2d ed. (Paderborn, 1892). On the text, see A. Baumstarck, *Die Vorlage des althochdeutschen Tatians,* rev. J. Rathofer (Cologne and Graz: Böhlau, 1964), J. fon Weringha, *Heliand und Diatessaron* (Assen: van Gorcum, 1965), and J. Rathofer, "Die Einwirkung des Fuldischen Evangelientextes auf den althochdeutschen Tatian," in: *Festschrift K. Langosch* (Darmstadt: WBG, 1973),

pp. 256–308. On the manuscript, see G. Baesecke, *Die Überlieferung des althochdeutschen Tatians* (Halle: Niemeyer, 1948).

21. See P. Ganz, "Ms. Junius 13 und die althochdeutsche Tatian-Übersetzung," *PBB* (Tübingen) 91 (1969):28–76, the research report by M. Schmidt, "Zum althochdeutschen Tatian," *Colloquia Germanica* 6 (1972):1–16, J. Rathofer's reply in the same journal, 7 (1973);55–57, and his papers "*Tatian und Fulda*," in the *Festschrift F. Tschirch,* ed. K.-H. Schirmer and B. Sowinski (Cologne: Böhlau, 1972), pp. 337–56, and "Ms. Junius 13 und die verschollene Tatian-Hs. B," *PBB* (Tübingen) 95 (1973):13–125.

22. On the language, see J. Lippert, *Beiträge zum Syntax althochdeutscher Übersetzungen* (Munich, 1974), who is critical of the notion of "faithful interpretation."

23. The edition cited is by H. Eggers, *Der althochdeutsche Isidor* (Tübingen, 1964). Facsimile in G. A. Hench, *Der althochdeutsche Isidor* (Strasbourg, 1893). For a recent study of the text, see K. Ostberg, *The Old High German Isidor* (Göppingen, 1979).

24. See K. Matzel, *Untersuchungen zur Verfasserschaft, Sprache und Herkunft der althochdeutschen Isidor-Sippe* (Bonn, 1970).

25. See G. Nordmeyer, "On the Old High German Isidor and Its Significance for Early German Prose Writing," *PMLA* 73 (1958):23–35, and R. Kienast, "Zur frühesten deutschen Kunstprosa," in: *Festschrift W. Stammler* (Berlin, 1953), pp. 11–24.

26. Ed. G. A. Hench, *The Monsee Fragments* (Strasbourg, 1890). See H. Plant, *Syntaktische Studien zu den Monseer Fragmenten* (Hague: Mouton, 1969), and on the Matthew problems, K. Matzel, "Der lateinische Text des Matthäusevangeliums der Monseer Fragmente," *PBB* (Tübingen) 87 (1965):289–363, as well as Lippert, *Syntax,* pp. 188–93.

Chapter Four

1. The history of medicine has a vast literature. The following may be useful: J. F. Payne, *English Medicine in the Anglo-Saxon Times* (Oxford: Clarendon Press, 1904); D. Riesman, *The Study of Medicine in the Middle Ages* (New York: Hoeber, 1936); J. Grattan and C. Singer, *Anglo-Saxon Magic and Medicine* (London: Oxford University Press, 1952); Z. Cope, *Sidelights on the History of Medicine* (London: Butterworth, 1957); W. Bonsen, *The Medical Background of Anglo-Saxon England* (London: Wellcome, 1963); G. Majno, *The Healing Hand* (Cambridge, Mass.: Harvard University Press, 1975).

2. See F. Genzmer, "Germanische Zaubersprüche," *Germanisch-Romanische Monatsschrift* 32 (1950):21–35; I. Bacon, "Versuch einer Klassifizierung altdeutscher Zaubersprüche und Segen," *MLN* 67 (1952):224–32; I. Hampp, "Vom Wesen des Zaubers im Zauberspruch," *Der Deutschunterricht* 13; no. 1 (1961):58–76.

3. The texts are in F. Wilhelm, *Denkmäler deutscher Prosa des 11. und 12.*

Jahrhunderts (Munich, 1916–18), pp. 39–42. There are elements of rhyme in the charm.

4. Genzmer, "Zaubersprüche," p. 24, notes the Indian parallels.

5. See F. Ködderitzsch, "Der zweite Merseburger Zauberspruch und seine Parallelen," *Zeitschrift für celtische Philologie* 33 (1974):45–57, has Gaelic and Indian examples.

6. Text in Wilhelm, *Denkmäler,* pp. 53–64. See in general A. Schirokauer, "Form und Formel einiger altdeutschen Zaubersprüche," *ZfdPh* 73 (1954):353–64.

7. See Eis, *Handschriften,* p. 26f., for a facsimile, and R. M. S. Heffner, "The Third Basel Recipe," *Journal of English and Germanic Philology* 46 (1947):248–53, for comments. On the use of honey, see Majno, *Healing Hand,* p. 50. For the medical interpretation, I am greatly indebted to Dr. C. Newman, librarian of the London Royal College of Physicians.

8. See, for example, Bacon, "Klassifizierung."

9. On the worm-charms, see G. Eis, *Altdeutsche Zaubersprüche* (Berlin, 1964), pp. 7–30. For later worm-charms invoking Job, see MSD XLVII/2a–b.

10. Facsimile in Fischer, *Schrifttafeln,* p. 16. A recent, although not particularly far-reaching, attempt to explain the presence of the charms is that by S. Fuller, "Pagan Charms in Tenth-Century Saxony?" *Monatshefte* 72 (1980):162–70.

11. There is an extensive literature. See Groseclose and Murdoch, *Denkmäler,* p. 52f. Phol has been seen as Apollo, St. Paul, or *vol* ("foal"), or as part of the words *volende* ("riding"), *vollente* ("perfect"), *valant* ("demon"), or *fol-henti* ("munificent"); *vuorun* has been read as *uuarun* ("were"), which alliterates with Wodan, who then becomes the singular subject of a plural verb.

12. A. Jacoby, *Ein bisher unbeachteter apokrypher Bericht über die Taufe Jesu* (Strasbourg: Trübner, 1902), and "Der Bamberger Blutsegen," *ZfdA* 54 (1913):200–209. F. Ohrt, *Die ältesten Segen über Christi Taufe* (Copenhagen: Levin and Munksgaard, 1938). On the blood-charms, see O. Erdmann, *Blut- und Wundsegen* (Berlin, 1903), and for texts, see the dissertation by C. Miller, "The Old High German and Old Saxon Charms" (Ph.D. Diss., Washington University, St. Louis, 1963).

13. G. Baesecke, "Contra caducum morbum," *PBB* 62 (1938):456–60, and T. Grienberger, "Contra caducum morbum," *PBB* 45 (1921):212–15.

14. See Eis, *Zaubersprüche,* pp. 88–108.

15. Wilhelm, *Denkmäler,* p. 51 (*Grazer Hagelsegen*).

16. See A. Schirokauer, "Der Eingang des Lorscher Bienensegens," *MLN* 57 (1942):62–65. Selected Anglo-Saxon charms are translated in R. K. Gordon, *Anglo-Saxon Poetry,* rev. ed. (London: Dent, 1954), pp. 85–94.

17. The first element of *chnospinci* may originally have been *chuo,* ("cow") and the blessing inscribed over a byre.

Chapter Five

1. See H. Uecker, *Germanische Heldensage* (Stuttgart, 1972). The poem of *Waltharius,* in Latin, by Ekkehart IV of St. Gallen, is translated by F. Genzmer, *Das Waltharilied* (Stuttgart: Reclam, 1953).

2. For summaries of criticism, see H. van der Kolk, *Das Hildebrandslied* (Amsterdam, 1967), and U. Schwab, *Arbeo laosa* (Berne, 1972). Two works with texts are worth noting: G. Baesecke, *Das Hildebrandlied* (Halle, 1945), and S. Gutenbrunner, *Von Hildebrand und Hadubrand* (Heidelberg, 1976).

3. W. F. Twaddell, "The Hildebrandslied Manuscript in the USA," *Journal of English and Germanic Philology* 73 (1974):157–68.

4. Fischer, *Schrifttafeln,* p. 12, is one of many facsimiles, the first made in 1729. On the manuscript, see H. Pongs, *Das Hildebrandslied* (Marburg, 1913).

5. F. Norman, *Three Essays on the Hildebrandslied,* ed. A. Hatto (London, 1973), p. 9.

6. See on the language such studies as Schwab, *Arbeo laosa,* and D. R. McLintock, "The Language of the *Hildebrandslied,*" *Oxford German Studies* 1 (1966):1–9.

7. W. Korgmann, *Das Hildebrandslied in der langobardischen Urfassung* (Berlin: Schmidt, 1959).

8. Gutenbrunner, *Von Hildebrand,* p. 139. My comment is not intended to detract from the value of Gutenbrunner's work, however.

9. I take issue here to an extent with D. R. McLintock's interesting paper on "The Politics of the *Hildebrandslied,*" *New German Studies* 2 (1974):61–81.

10. Of the many studies on the saga, two recent papers only may be cited here: W. Hoffmann, "Das *Hildebrandslied* und die indogermanischen Vater-Sohn-Kampf-Dichtungen," *PBB* (Tübingen) 92 (1970):26–42, and A. T. Hatto, "On the Excellence of the *Hildebrandslied,*" *Modern Language Review* 68 (1973):820–38. See also W. Harms, *Der Kampf mit dem Freund oder nahem Verwandten* (Munich: Fink, 1963), pp. 18–33.

11. See such standard works as C. M. Bowra, *Heroic Poetry* (London: Macmillan, 1952), and A. B. Lord, *The Singer of Tales* (Cambridge, Mass.: Harvard University Press, 1960).

12. See K. v. See, *Germanische Verskunst* (Stuttgart, 1967), and W. Hoffmann, *Altdeutsche Metrik* (Stuttgart, 1967), and now D. R. McLintock, "Metre and Rhythm in the *Hildebrandslied,*" *Modern Language Review* 71 (1976):565–76.

13. See Schwab, *Arbeo laosa.* Critics have warned against reading too much into the phrase: McLintock, "Politics," p. 63.

14. There is a summary of the views in S. Beyschlag, "Hiltibrant enti Hadubrant," in: *Festschrift für L. L. Hammerich* (Copenhagen: Naturmetodens Sproginstitut, 1962), pp. 13–28, and van der Kolk, *Hildebrandslied,* has a chart, p. 116.

15. Translated by P. Terry in *Poems of the Vikings* (Indianapolis and New York: Bobbs-Merrill, 1969), p. 24.

Chapter Six

1. Facsimile in Fischer, *Schrifttafeln*, p. 14. See U. Schwab, *Die Sternrune im Wessobrunner Gebet* (Amsterdam, 1973).

2. See P. F. Ganz, "Die Zeilenaufteilung im *Wessobrunner Gebet*," *PBB* (Tübingen) 95 (1973: Festschrift I. Schröbler):39–51; and N. Voorwinden, "Das *Wessobrunner Gebet*," *Neophilologus* 59 (1975):390–404.

3. See Bostock, *Handbook*, pp. 127–35, on the language. Ganz, "Zeilenaufteilung," considers that the line-division points and abbreviations for "and" (italicized in the text) may be joined as a kind of paragraphing sign. Some abbreviations could be lost without damage to the work.

4. See E. R. Friesse, "The Form of the *Wessobrunn Prayer II*," *Modern Language Review* 50 (1955):317–19, and L. Seiffert, "The Metrical Form and Composition of the *Wessobrunner Gebet*," *Medium Aevum* 31 (1962):1–13. The text is from Steinmeyer, but the poetic second part follows Mettke, *Älteste Dichtung*, p. 156, where there is also a translation.

5. There is no reason why there should not be actual verbal links even with Old Norse. But the link is strictly verbal, and implies nothing about the nature of the work as a whole.

6. See Ehrismann, *Geschichte* . . . 1:144.

7. Facsimile in Fischer, *Schrifttafeln*, p. 16, and close-ups of some of the text in C. Minis, *Handschrift, Form und Sprache des Muspilli* (Berlin, 1966).

8. On the linguistic difficulties, see R. Bergmann, "Zum Problem der Sprache des *Muspilli*," *Frühmittelalterliche Studien* 5 (1971):304–15, and the general comments by Haug and Mohr, *Zweimal Muspilli.*

9. G. Baesecke, "Muspilli II," *ZfdA* 82 (1948/50):199–239. Supporters and critics are summarized in Rupp, *Forschung*, p. 56.

10. See Minis, *Handschrift*, for comments on the unity of the work, although his structural comments are less convincing, as well as the joint volume by Haug and Mohr, *Zweimal Muspilli.*

11. On legal aspects, see H. Kolb, "*Vora demo muspille*," *ZfdPh* 83 (1964):2–33, and "Himmlisches und irdisches Gericht in karolingischer Theologie," *Frühmittelalterliche Studien* 5 (1971):284–303. On overdoing this aspect, see H. Finger, *Untersuchungen zum Muspilli* (Göppingen, 1977), pp. 106–21.

12. See H. W. Sommer, "The *Muspilli*-Apocalypse," *Germanic Review* 35 (1960):157–63, and "The Pseudepigraphic Source of '*Muspilli II*,'" *Monatshefte* 55 (1963):107–12. There is a full study by W. Kettler, *Das Jüngste Gericht* (Berlin, 1977), which is of general interest, as is D. Dumville, "Biblical Apocrypha and the Early Irish," *Proceedings of the Royal Irish Academy* 73(c) (1973):299–338: see p. 309.

13. Translated in Gordon, *Anglo-Saxon Poetry*, p. 150. See Finger, *Untersuchungen*, pp. 183–91, on the relationship.

14. G. N. Garmondsway, *The Anglo-Saxon Chronicle* (London: Dent, 1953), pp. 236, 263. See in general Schlosser, *Anfänge*, pp. 70–74, Finger, *Untersuchungen*, p. 194f., and the conclusions of both Haug and Mohr, *Zweimal Muspilli*.

Chapter Seven

1. *Heliand*, ed. E. Sievers (Halle, 1878); *Heliand und Genesis*, ed. O. Behaghel; 8th ed. W. Mitzka (Tübingen, 1965). Text cited from the latter. There is a modern German version by F. Genzmer, *Heliand* (Stuttgart: Reclam, 1966), and an English version by M. Scott, *The Heliand* (Chapel Hill: University of North Carolina Press, 1966). There is a bibliography by J. Belkin and J. Meier, *Bibliographie zu Otfrid . . . und zur altsächsischen Bibeldichtung* (Berlin, 1975), pp. 61–131. Three collections of essays in the Darmstadt Wissenschaftliche *Buchgesellschaft* series *Wege der Forschung* are of value in this chapter, and references will be made to articles in them as far as possible: J. Eichhoff and I. Rauch, *Der Heliand* (Darmstadt, 1973), W. Kleiber, *Otfrid von Weissenburg* (Darmstadt, 1978), and U. Ernst and P.-E. Neuser, *Die Genese der europäischen Endreimdichtung* (Darmstadt, 1977). These will be referred to as *WdF/Heliand, WdF/Otfrid,* and *WdF/Endreim,* respectively.

2. The soures are summarized in W. Huber, *Heliand und Matthäus-Exegese* (Munich, 1969), pp. 12–58.

3. A. Masser, *Bibel- und Legendenepik des deutschen Mittelalters* (Berlin: Schmidt, 1976), p. 23.

4. The controversial topic of numerical structure in the *Heliand* cannot be treated in a book on Old High German, although reference will be made to tectonic problems in Otfrid, themselves in some respects equally controversial.

5. The major study is that by W. Kleiber, *Otfrid von Weissenburg* (Berne and Munich, 1974). See also W. Haubrichs, "Eine prosopographische Skizze zu Otfrid," in: *WdF/Otfrid,* pp. 397–413.

6. There is a full facsimile of the Vienna codex, edited by H. Butzmann (Graz, 1972), and many facsimiles in Kleiber's study of Otfrid.

7. Major editions are by J. Kelle, *Otfrids . . . Evangelienbuch* (Regensburg, 1856–81); P. Piper, *Otfrids Evangelienbuch,* 2d ed. (Tübingen and Freiburg/Br., 1882–87)—the only text to take the Heidelberg manuscript as its basis; O. Erdmann, *Otfrids Evangelienbuch* (Halle, 1882). The last-noted served as the basis for the study-text, 6th ed. by L. Wolff (Tübingen, 1973), which is cited here. Translation by J. Kelle, *Christi Leben* (Prague, 1870; reprinted Osnabrück: Zeller, 1966).

8. Note in particular the papers by H. Brinkmann and H. Rupp in *WdF/Endreim,* as well as S. Gutenbrunner, "Otfrid über Poesie und Prosa," *ZfdA* 96 (1967):69–73. A full study is that by R. Patzlaff, *Otfrid von Weissenburg und die*

mittelalterliche versus-Tradition (Tübingen, 1975). On the meter in general, see Hoffmann, *Metrik*.

9. See for example H. Klingenberg, "Zum Grundriß der althochdeutschen Evangeliendichtung Otfrids," *ZfdA* 99 (1970):35–45, and 101 (1972):229–43, several of the papers in the *WdF/Otfrid,* and Kleiber, *Otfrid.* W. Haubrichs, *Ordo also Form* (Tübingen: Niemeyer, 1969), caused some controversy: see the reviews by W. Schröder, *PBB* (Tübingen) 94 (1972):439–46, and U. Schwab, *Studi Medievali* 12 (1971):277–300.

10. C. Soeteman, *Untersuchungen zur Übersetzungstechnik Otfrid von Weissenburgs* (Groningen: University, 1939); H. A. Kissel, *Untersuchungen zu Möglichkeiten, Umfang und Typologie verbaler Synonymik bei Otfried* (Berne and Frankfurt/M.: Lang, 1975); K. Schulz, *Art und Herkunft des variierenden Stils* (Munich, 1968).

11. D. A. McKenzie, *Otfrid von Weissenburg: Narrator or Commentator* (Stanford and London, 1946).

12. R. Hartmann, *Allegorisches Wörterbuch zu Otfrieds . . . Evangeliendichtung* (Munich, 1975). Other important studies are those by U. Ernst, *Der Liber Evangeliorum* (Cologne and Vienna, 1975), G. Vollmann-Profe, *Kommentar zu Otfrids Evangelienbuch I.* (Bonn, 1976) and P. Michel and A. Schwarz, *Unz in obanentig* (Bonn, 1978).

13. Facsimile in Fischer, *Schrifttafeln,* p. 21.

14. See J. K. Bostock's review of McKenzie, *Narrator,* in *Medium Aevum* 16 (1947):53–57. On the origins, see F. Maurer, "Zur Frage nach der Heimat des Gedichtes von Christus und der Samariterin," *ZfdPh* 54 (1929):175–79.

15. See two papers by H. Rupp: "Otfrid . . . und die spätantike Bibeldichtung," *PBB* (Tübingen) 86 (1964):138–47, and *WdF/Endreim,* and: "Über das Verhältnis von deutscher und lateinischer Dichtung im 9.–12. Jahrhundert," *Germanisch-Romanische Monatsschrift* 39 (1958):19–34. Also R. Gasser, "Propter lamentabilem vocem hominis," *Freiburger Zeitschrift für Philosophie und Theologie* 19 (1970):3–83, and G. Meissburger, *Grundlagen zum Verständnis der deutschen Mönchsdichtung im 11. und 12. Jahrhundert* (Munich, 1970), pp. 65–80.

Chapter Eight

1. R. Bergmann, "Zu der althochdeutschen Inschrift aus Köln," *RVjb* 30 (1965):66–69, with a picture of the map.

2. Facsimile in Fischer, *Schrifttafeln,* p. 20. See L. Stavenhagen, "Das *Petruslied,*" *Wirkendes Wort* 17 (1967):21–28, and K. Gamber, "Das altbairische *Petruslied,*" in: *Festschrift für F. Haberl* (Regensburg, 1977), pp. 107–16.

3. See J. Müller-Blattau, "Zur Form und Überlieferung der ältesten deutschen geistlichen Lieder," *Zeitschrift für Musikwissenschaft* 17 (1935):129–46; O. Ursprung, "Das Freisinger *Petruslied,*" *Die Musikforschung* 5

(1952):17–21, and H. Hucke, "Die Neumierung des althochdeutschen *Petruslieds*," in: *Festschrift für J. S. van Waesberghe* (Amsterdam: IMM, 1963), pp. 71–78.

4. See W. Mettin, "Die ältesten deutschen Pilgerlieder," in: *Festschrift E. Sievers* (Halle: Niemeyer, 1896), pp. 227–86.

5. E. Jammers, "Das mittelalterliche deutsche Epos und die Musik," *Heidelberger Jahrbuch* (1957):85.

6. Facsimile in Fischer, *Schrifttafeln,* p. 23, and in H. Menhardt, "Zur Überlieferung des althochdeutschen 138. Psalms," *ZfdA* 77 (1940):76–84.

7. The closest to this arrangement is that given by Menhardt, "Überlieferung." Most texts insist on the manuscript order, though MSD has two-lines strophes only.

8. O. Ludwig, "Der althochdeutsche und der biblische Psalm 138," *Euphorion* 56 (1962):402–9.

Chapter Nine

1. Fischer's facsimile is only partial: see M. Enneccerus, *Versbau und gesanglicher Vortrag des ältesten französischen Liedes* (Frankfurt/M.: Enneccerus, 1901), for a full one. See too the text by R. Schützeichel in E. Berg, "Das *Ludwigslied* und die Schlacht bei Saucourt," *RVjb* 29 (1964):197–99. On the language, see E. Urmoneit, *Der Wortschatz des Ludwigsliedes* (Munich, 1973).

2. On the historical background, see Berg, "Schlacht," and R. Harvey, "The Provenance of the Old High German *Ludwigslied*," *Medium Aevum* 14 (1945):1–20; R. Schützeichel, "Das Heil des Königs," *PBB* (Tübingen) 94 (1972: Festschrift für H. Eggers):369–91; B. Murdoch, "Saucourt and the *Ludwigslied*," *Revue Belge de Philologie et d'Histoire* 55 (1977):841–67. On Hincmar: G. Ehrenforth, "Hinkmar von Rheims und Ludwig III von Westfranken," *Zeitschrift für Kirchengeschichte* 44 (1925):65–98.

3. H. Homann, "Das *Ludwigslied*—Dichtung im Dienste der Politik?" in: *Studies in Honor of H. Jantz* (Munich, 1972), pp. 17–28. See also R. Kemper, "Das *Ludwigslied* im Kontext zeitgenössischer Rechtsvorgänge," *Deutsche Vierteljahresschrift* 56 (1982):161–77.

4. F. Willems, "Der parataktische Satzstil im *Ludwigslied*," *ZfdA* 85 (1954/5):18–35.

5. See the fascinating account by the Valenciennes librarian P. Lefranq, *Rhythmus Teutonicus ou Ludwigslied?* (Paris: Droz, 1945). In 1968 R. Combridge noted that the word printed as *frâno* in line 46 actually reads *frôno*, the expected High German form: "Zur Handschrift des *Ludwigsliedes*," *ZfdA* 97 (1968):33–37.

6. R. Schützeichel, "Das *Ludwigslied* und die Erforschung des Westfränkischen," *RVjb* 31 (1966/7):291–306.

7. A. Heusler, *Die altgermanische Dichtung,* 2d ed. (Potsdam: Athenaion, 1943), p. 122f.

8. M. Wehrli, "Gattungsgeschichtliche Betrachtungen zum *Ludwigslied*," now available in his *Formen mittelalterlicher Erzählung* (Zurich and Freiburg/Br., 1969), pp. 73–86. See too the earlier dissertation by H. Naumann, *Das Ludwigslied und die verwandten lateinischen Gedichte* (Halle, 1932), and more recently H. Beck, "Zur literaturgeschichtliche Stellung des althochdeutschen *Ludwigslieds*," *ZfdA* 103 (1974):37–51.

9. Fischer, *Schrifttafeln*, p. 24, shows the manuscript. On the language see H. Christensen, "Das althochdeutsche Gedicht *De Heinrico*," *Kopenhagener Beiträge zur germanistischen Linguistik* 10 (1978):18–32. On the background of the work, see W. Jungandreas, "*De Heinrico*," *Leuvense Bijdragen* 57 (1968):75–91; with different views: M. Uhlirz, "Der modus *De Heinrico* und sein geschichtlicher Inhalt," *Deutsche Vierteljahresschrift* 26 (1952): 153–61, and M.-L. Dittrich, "*De Heinrico*," *ZfdA* 84 (1952/3):274–308 (postulating a Bavarian original).

10. There are no full facsimiles available, and that in Fischer, *Schrifttafeln*, p. 19, is of a few lines only. On the language, see Bostock, *Handbook*, pp. 227–30, and on Wisolf, F. Tschirch, "Wisolf, eine mittelalterliche Schreiberpersönlichkeit," *PBB* (Halle) 73 (1961):387–422. The complexity of the orthography seems to indicate that dyslexia is not the answer, however appealing this might seem. The form of the name *Gorio* is acceptable.

11. The most recent discussion of the legends is that by W. Haubrichs, *Georgslied und Georgslegende* (Königstein im Taunus, 1977).

12. The best-known later version is probably that of the *Golden Legend* of Jacobus de Voragine, tr. G. Ryan and H. Ripperger (New York and London: Longmans, 1941), pp. 232–38. The dragon episode, probably adapted directly from the Perseus and Andromeda story, is simply placed before the passion. Even early vernacular versions of the legend complain from time to time that "untrue" elements have been added. The links with Christ are explored by F. Tschirch, "Der heilige Georg als figura Christi," *Festschrift H. de Boor* (Tübingen: Niemeyer, 1966), pp. 1–19.

13. H. Brauer, "Die Heidelberger Handschrift von Otfrids *Evangelienbuch* und das althochdeutsche *Georgslied*," *ZfdPh* 55 (1930):261–68.

Chapter Ten

1. See Ehrismann, *Geschichte* . . . 1:364–94, for details of smaller Latin poems, the beast-epic *Ecbasis Capitivi* [Escape of a Captive], and the writings of Hrotsvita of Gandersheim. It is impossible to include, too, the Latin sequences of Notker I of St. Gallen.

2. The text is in MSD vol. II, 103f. See P. Dronke, *Medieval Latin and the Rise of European Love Lyric*, 2d ed. (Oxford, 1968), 2:353–56, for a text with reconstructed opening.

3. A convenient text is that edited by F. P. Knapp with a translation: *Ruodlieb* (Stuttgart, 1977). The passage is in book XVII, lines 12f. and 67f.

4. Sonderegger, *Althochdeutsch in St. Gallen,* p. 72.

5. Ibid., p. 74f.

6. Ibid., pp. 72–74.

7. T. Frings, "Hirsch und Hinde," *PBB* (Halle) 85 (1963):22–26. Ehrismann, *Geschichte* . . . 1:243f. See Groseclose and Murdoch, *Denkmäler,* p. 98f., for a summary of views.

8. See U. Schwab, "Eber, aper und porcus in Notkers des Deutschen *Rhetorik,*" *Annali dell'Istituto Orientale di Napoli* (Sezione Linguistica) 8 (1967):1–25.

9. Text in E. Schröder, "Die Tänzer von Kölbigk," *Zeitschrift für Kirchengeschichte* 17 (1897):94–164, with a study by K. Borck, "Der Tanz zu Kölbigk," *PBB* 76 (1954):241–320. On the snowflake riddle, see Eis, *Zaubersprüche,* pp. 67–76.

10. See P. J. Diamant, "Althochdeutsches Schlummerlied," *Jahrbuch des Leo-Baeck-Instituts* 5 (1960):338–45.

Chapter Eleven

1. Three editions of Notker need noting: P. Piper, *Die Schriften Notkers* (Freiburg/Br. and Leipzig, 1883–95); E. H. Sehrt and T. Starck, *Notkers des Deutschen Werke* (Halle, 1933–55)—edited for the *Altdeutsche Textbibliothek* series and incomplete; and a new edition for the same series, now in progress (since 1972), although published in Tübingen, edited by J. C. King and P. Tax. This exemplary edition also provides illustrations of the manuscripts, and has a subsidiary section called *Notker Latinus,* either published separately or as insert booklets, with Notker's Latin sources. But all three editions need to be consulted. The letter to Hugo is in Piper, *Notker,* 1:859–61, and there is a translation in Ehrismann, *Geschichte* . . ., 1:421f.

2. Space precludes details of the numerous language studies, although there are various dictionaries to the works. See E. S. Coleman, however, on "Die Lehnbildungen in Notkers Übersetzungen," *Taylor Starck Festschrift* (The Hague: Mouton, 1964), pp. 106–29.

3. Cited from the Sehrt/Starck edition of the Psalter, *Notker* 3/ii:533.

4. See A. L. Lloyd, *The Manuscripts and Fragments of Notkers Psalter* (Giessen, 1958). Lloyd has also edited *Der Münchener Psalter des 14. Jahrhunderts* (Berlin: Schmidt, 1969).

5. Notker's methods are summed up by S. Sonderegger in his interesting paper "Gesprochene Sprache im Althochdeutschen," in: *Ansätze zu einer pragmatischen Sprachgeschichte,* ed. H. Sitta (Tübingen, 1980), pp. 71–88. For the sources of the Psalm commentaries, see the *Notker Latinus* volumes to the Psalter, in the King and Tax edition, vols. 8a, 9a, and 10a.

6. Sehrt/Starck, *Notker* 3/iii:1057–1117.

7. All three editions have the text: King/Tax is vol. 4 (1979).

8. Sehrt/Starck, *Notker* 1/i. The citation is on p. 9. See H. R. Patch, *The Tradition of Boethius* (New York: Oxford University Press, 1935).

9. The two works are vols. 5 and 6 of the King-Tax edition, each with accompanying *Latinus*. Citation on p. 4 of the latter.

10. Texts are in Piper, *Notker,* 1:cxlix and 591–684.

11. Piper, *Notker,* 1:851–59.

12. The standard text is now E. H. Bartelmez, *The Expositio in Cantica Canticorum of Williram* (Philadelphia, 1967), cited here by biblical chapter and verse. See V. Schupp, *Studien zu Williram von Ebersberg* (Berne and Munich, 1978). On the St. Trudpert text, see F. Ohly, *Hohelied-Studien* (Wiesbaden: Steiner, 1958). It is edited by H. Menhardt, *Das St Trudperter Hohelied* (Halle: Niemeyer, 1934).

13. *Deutsche Sprachgeschichte II. Das Mittelhochdeutsche* (Reinbek bei Hamburg, 1965), p. 46.

14. The Vienna Notker is in the Piper edition, vol. 3.

15. See D. R. McLintock, *"Himmel und Hölle,"* in: *Studien zur frühmittelhochdeutschen Literatur,* ed. L. P. Johnson et al. (Berlin, 1974), pp. 83–102, on the language.

16. See Bischoff, "St Emmeram," for details of Otloh's work in general, as well as W. Schröder, "Der Geist von Cluny und die Anfänge des frühmittelhochdeutschen Schrifttums," *PBB* 72 (1952):371–82.

Chapter Twelve

1. *Geschichte . . . II* (1922), p. 1.

2. See C. Soeteman, *Deutsche geistliche Dichtung des 11. und 12. Jahrhunderts,* 2d ed. (Stuttgart, 1971), and H. Rupp, *Deutsche religiöse Dichtungen des 11. u. 12 Jahrhunderts,* 2d ed. (Berne and Munich, 1971), as well as Meissburger, *Mönchsdichtung* (with important review by W. Schröder, *ZfdA* 100 [1971]:195–213.)

3. See F. Maurer's *Die religiösen Dichtungen des 11. und 12. Jahrhunderts* (Tübingen, 1964–70), and W. Schröder's review articles, *PBB* (Tübingen) 88 (1967):249–84, and 93 (1971):109–38.

4. Discussed above, Chapter 4.

5. Ed. G. Mellbourn (Lund and Copenhagen: Gleerup, 1944), p. 37.

6. *Die frühmittelhochdeutsche Wiener Genesis,* ed. K. Smits (Berlin: Schmidt, 1972). See lines 524–26.

7. J. Diemer, *Deutsche Gedichte des XI. und XII. Jahrhunderts* (Vienna, 1849), p. 10.

8. See P. Dronke, *The Medieval Lyric* (London: Hutchinson, 1968), p. 49.

9. *Religiöse Dichtungen,* pp. 51f., 55–59.

10. R. Schützeichel, *Das alemannische Memento Mori* (Tübingen: Niemeyer, 1962), has a text, facsimile, and discussion.

11. Texts in Maurer, *Dichtungen*, 2:134–39, 369–513. The edition of the *Kaiserchronik* is that by E. Dümmler (1892; repr. Dublin: Weidmann, 1969).

12. Text and translation ed. E. Nellmann, *Das Annolied* (Stuttgart: Reclam, 1975). See D. Knab, *Das Annolied* (Tübingen: Niemeyer, 1962), and A. Haverkamp, *Typik und Politik im Annolied* (Stuttgart: Metzler, 1979).

13. D. Kartschoke, *Das Rolandslied des Pfaffen Konrad* (Fischer: Frankfurt/ M., 1970), has a text and translation.

14. N. T. J. Voorwinden, *Merigarto* (Leiden: Leiden University Press, 1973).

15. Later texts are in Maurer, *Dichtungen*, 1:169–245. See N. Henkel, *Studien zum Physiologus im Mittelalter* (Tübingen: Niemeyer, 1976). On the unicorn, see J. Einhorn, *Spiritalis unicornis* (Munich: Fink, 1976), giving an idea of the breadth of the tradition.

Selected Bibliography

The primary and secondary literature of Old High German is enormous. This list is very selective indeed, noting for reasons of space only works likely to be the most useful. Considerations of space have led to the exclusion of standard reference works like the *Verfasserlexikon* and of most literary histories.

PRIMARY SOURCES

1. Anthologies

Ahd. G1.; Lb.; MSD.; St. See "Abbreviations" for details.

Daab, U. *Drei Reichenauer Denkmäler der altalemannischen Frühzeit.* Tübingen: Niemeyer, 1963.

Gernentz, H. J. *Althochdeutsche Literatur.* Berlin: Union, 1979.

Heyne, M. *Kleinere altniederdeutsche Denkmäler.* Paderborn, 1877; reprint Amsterdam: Rodopi, 1970.

Maurer, F. *Die religiösen Dichtungen des 11. und 12. Jahrhunderts.* Tübingen; Niemeyer, 1964–70.

Mettke, H. *Altdeutsche Texte.* Leipzig: Bibliographisches Institut, 1970.

———. *Älteste deutsche Dichtung und Prosa.* Leipzig: Reclam, 1976.

Miller, C. *The Old High German and Old Saxon Charms.* Ph.D. Diss., Washington University, St. Louis, 1963 (typescript).

Schlosser, H. D. *Althochdeutsche Literatur.* Frankfurt/M. and Hamburg: Fischer, 1970; new edition: 1980.

Wilhelm, F. *Denkmäler deutscher Prosa des 11. und 12. Jahrhunderts.* Munich, 1916–18; reprint Munich: Hueber, 1960.

2. Individual Texts

Abrogans. *Der deutsche Abrogans.* Edited by G. Baesecke. Halle: Niemeyer, 1931.

Arator-Glosses. *Die althochdeutschen Aratorglossen der Handschrift Trier 1464.* Edited by H. von Gadow. Munich: Fink, 1974.

Benedictine Rule. *Die althochdeutsche Benediktinerregel des Cod. Sang. 916.* Edited by U. Daab. Tübingen: Niemeyer, 1959.

146

Heliand. *Heliand.* Edited by E. Sievers. Halle: Waisenhaus, 1878. *Heliand und Genesis.* Edited by O. Behaghel; 8th edited by W. Mitzka. Tübingen: Niemeyer, 1965.

Isidor. *Der althochdeutsche Isidor.* Edited by H. Eggers. Tübingen: Niemeyer, 1964.

Monsee Fragments. *The Monsee Fragments.* Edited by G. A. Hench. Strasbourg: Trübner, 1890.

Murbach Hymns. *Die Murbacher Hymnen.* Edited by E. Sievers. Halle, 1874; reprint ed. edited by E. S. Firchow. New York and London: Johnson, 1972.

Notker. *Die Schriften Notkers.* Edited by P. Piper. Freiburg/Br. and Leipzig: Mohr, 1883–95. *Die Werke Notkers des Deutschen.* Edited by E. H. Sehrt and T. Starck. Halle: Niemeyer, 1933–55. *Die Werke Notkers* . . . Neue Ausgabe. Edited by J. C. King and P. Tax. Tübingen: Niemeyer, 1972ff.

Otfrid. *Otfrids . . . Evangelienbuch.* Edited by J. Kelle. Regensburg, 1856–81; reprint Aalen: Zeller, 1963. *Otfrids Evangelienbuch.* Edited by P. Piper. 2d ed. Freiburg/Br. and Tübingen: Mohr, 1882–87. *Otfrids . . . Evangelienbuch.* Edited by O. Erdmann. Halle, 1882; reprint Hildesheim: Olms, 1979. *Studienausgabe* of Erdmann's edition. 6th ed. edited by L. Wolff. Tübingen: Niemeyer, 1973.

Summarium Heinrici. *Summarium Heinrici.* Edited by R. Hildebrandt. Berlin and New York: de Gruyter, 1974ff. In progress: vol I (1974), vol II (1982).

Tatian. *Tatian.* Edited by E. Sievers. 2d ed. Paderborn, 1892; reprint Paderborn: Schöningh, 1966.

Williram. *The Expositio in Cantica Canticorum of Williram.* Edited by E. H. Bartlemez. Philadelphia: American Philosophical Soc., 1967.

3. Facsimiles

Baesecke, G. *Lichtdrucke nach althochdeutschen Handschriften.* Halle: Niemeyer, 1926.

Bischoff, B., Duft, J., and Sonderegger, S. *Das älteste deutsche Buch. Die Abrogans-Handschrift der Stiftsbibliothek St Gallen.* St. Gallen: Zollikofer, 1977.

Butzmann, H. *Vollständige Faksimile-Ausgabe des Codex Vindobonensis 2687.* Graz: Akademie, 1972. Otfrid's *Evangelienbuch.*

Eis, G. *Altdeutsche Handschiften.* Munich: Beck, 1949.

Fischer, H. *Schrifttafeln zum althochdeutschen Lesebuch.* Tübingen: Niemeyer, 1966.

Hench, G. *Der althochdeutsche Isidor.* Strasbourg: Trübner, 1893.

4. Grammars and Dictionaries

Braune, W. *Althochdeutsche Grammatik.* 13th ed. Edited by H. Eggers. Tübingen: Niemeyer, 1975.

Eggers, H. *Vollständiges lateinisch-althochdeutsches Wörterbuch zur . . . Isidor-Übersetzung.* Berlin: Akademie, 1960.

Graff, E. H. *Althochdeutscher Sprachschatz.* Berlin, 1834–46; reprint Darmstadt: WBG, 1963. The last volume is an index by H. Massmann which serves as a *Gedrängtes Wörterbuch.*

Karg-Gasterstädt, E., and Frings, T. *Althochdeutsches Wörterbuch.* Leipzig and Berlin: Akademie, 1952ff.

Köhler, F. *Lateinisch-althochdeutsches Glossar zur Tatian-Übersetzung.* Paderborn, 1914; reprint Paderborn: Schöningh, 1962.

Massmann, H. F. See Graff, above.

Schützeichel, R. *Althochdeutsches Wörterbuch.* 2d ed. Tübingen: Niemeyer, 1974.

Sehrt, E. *Notker-Glossar.* Tübingen: Niemeyer, 1962.

———. *Vollständiges Wörterbuch zum Heliand und zur altsächsischen Genesis.* 2d ed. Göttingen: Vandenhoeck and Ruprecht, 1966.

Starck, T., and Wells, J. C. *Althochdeutsches Glossenwörterbuch.* Heidelberg: Winter, 1972 ff.

SECONDARY SOURCES

1. Bibliographies and Bibliographical Handbooks

Belkin, J., and Meier, J. *Bibliographie zu Otfrid von Weissenburg und zur altsächsischen Bibeldichtung.* Berlin: Erich Schmidt, 1975. Full and up-to-date listing of material. The older editions have bibliographies of early studies.

Bergmann, R. *Verzeichnis der althochdeutschen und altsächsischen Glossenhandschriften.* Berlin and New York: de Gruyter, 1973. The major reference listing of the glosses. Additions have already been made. See Mayer, below.

Groseclose, J. S., and Murdoch, B. O. *Die althochdeutschen poetischen Denkmäler.* Stuttgart: Metzler, 1976. Discussion and bibliography of the rhymed and alliterative texts.

Hoffmann, W. *Altdeutsche Metrik.* Stuttgart: Metzler, 1967. A handbook on metrics as well as a bibliographical guide.

Kartschoke, D. *Altdeutsche Bibeldichtung.* Stuttgart: Metzler, 1975. On High and Low German texts. Complements Groseclose/Murdoch.

van der Kolk, H. *Das Hildebrandslied. Eine forschungsgeschichtliche Darstellung.* Amsterdam: Scheltema and Holkema, 1967. The fullest discursive study of *Hildebrandslied* research.

Mayer, H. *Althochdeutsche Glossen: Nachtrag.* Toronto and Buffalo: University of Toronto Press, 1974. Supplements Bergmann, above.

Rupp, H. *Forschung zur althochdeutschen Literatur 1945–1962.* Stuttgart: Metzler, 1965. A good survey of research (reprinted from the *Deutsche Vierteljahrsschrift*), although emphases have shifted since it was written.

von See, K. *Germanische Verskunst.* Stuttgart: Metzler, 1967. Detailed discussion and bibliography of alliterative verse.

Soeteman, C. *Deutsche geistliche Dichtung des 11. und 12. Jahrhunderts.* 2d ed. Stuttgart: Metzler, 1971. Very useful handbook/bibliography of the extensive religious poetry of the early Middle High German period.

Uecker, H. *Germanische Heldensage.* Stuttgart: Metzler, 1972. Useful for *Hildebrandslied* and for details of lost poetry.

2. Books

Baesecke, G. *Der deutsche Abrogans und die Herkunft des althochdeutschen Schrifttums.* Halle: Niemeyer, 1930. An important study of the glosses in general, with numerous illustrations.

————. *Das Hildebrandlied.* Halle: Niemeyer, 1945. A sober textual reconstruction and discussion.

————. *Kleinere Schriften zur althochdeutschen Sprache und Literatur,* ed. W. Schröder. Berne and Munich: Francke, 1966. Very useful collection of many of Baesecke's most important contributions, especially on the glosses, with interesting afterword.

Bertau, K. *Deutsche Literatur im europäischen Mittelalter.* Munich: Beck, 1972–73. Literature in historical and social contexts. The sparseness of the Old High German remains becomes clear.

Bostock, J. K. *A Handbook on Old High German Literature.* 2d ed. Edited by K. C. King and D. R. McLintock. Oxford: Clarendon Press, 1976. The major English-language study of the literature, updated and revised. Excellent on questions of language.

Daab, U. *Studien zur althochdeutschen Benediktinerregel.* Halle, 1929; reprint Walluf: Sändig, 1973. Language, sources, text.

Dronke, P. *Medieval Latin and the Rise of the European Love-Lyric.* 2d ed. Oxford; Oxford University Press, 1968. Contains texts and studies, with good material on *Suavissima nonna.*

Eggers, H. *Deutsche Sprachgeschichte.* Reinbek bei Hamburg: Rowohlt, 1963–77. Vols. 1 and 2 of this 4-volume set cover our period; a readable literary, not just philological, survey.

Ehrismann, G. *Geschichte der deutschen Literatur bis zum Ausgang des Mittelalters.* 2d ed. Munich, 1922–34; reprint Munich: Beck, 1954. See vols. 1 and 2/i. Outdated, and idiosyncratic on some of the smaller texts, this is still a useful handbook. The "new beginning" implied in 2/i is no longer accepted, however.

Eichhoff, J., and Rauch, I., eds. *Der Heliand.* Darmstadt: WBG, 1973. A good collection of major essays in the *Wege der Forschung* series (no. 321) of the *Wissenschaftliche Buchgesellschaft.*

Eis, G. *Altdeutsche Zaubersprüche*. Berlin: de Gruyter, 1964. Collection of essays, not all on early material, but demonstrating the continuity of this type of text.

Erdmann, O. *Blut- und Wundsegen in ihrer Entwicklung dargestellt*. Berlin: Mayer and Müller, 1903. Full comparative survey.

Ernst, U. *Der Liber Evangeliorum Otfrids von Weissenburg*. Cologne and Vienna: Böhlau, 1975. A major full-length study.

Ernst, U., and Neuser, P.-E., eds. *Die Genese der europäischen Endreimdichtung*. Darmstadt: WBG, 1977. A collection of essays of very considerable importance to the study of Otfrid. *Wege der Forschung* 444.

Finger, W. *Untersuchungen zum Muspilli*. Göppingen: Kümmerle, 1977. A full study, with evaluations of earlier views.

Gutenbrunner, S. *Von Hildebrand und Hadubrand. Lied-Sage-Mythos*. Heidelberg: Winter, 1976. A very full (sometimes even a little too full) investigation of the Hildebrand plot.

Hartmann, R. *Allegorisches Wörterbuch zu Otfrieds . . . Evangeliendichtung*. Munich: Fink, 1975. A massive handbook of the exegetical ideas used in Otfrid's writing.

Haubrichs, W. *Georgslied und Georgslegende im frühen Mittelalter*. Königsstein im Taunus: Scriptor, 1977. Extensive background study.

Hellgardt, E. *Die exegetischen Quellen von Otfrids Evangelienbuch*. Tübingen: Niemeyer, 1981.

Huber, W. *Heliand und Matthäusexegese*. Munich: Hueber, 1969. Interesting study of all the sources for the *Heliand*.

Kettler, W. *Das Jüngste Gericht*. Berlin and New York: de Gruyter, 1977. Useful for *Muspilli*.

King, K. C. *The Earliest German Monasteries*. Nottingham: University Inaugural Lecture, 1961. Brief but very useful survey.

Kleiber, W. *Otfrid von Weissenburg*. Berne and Munich: Francke, 1971. The major independent study of Otfrid's life and work, and on the Weissenburg scriptorium. Do not confuse with:

———., ed. *Otfrid von Weissenburg*. Darmstadt: WBG, 1978. Introduction and collection of important essays. *Wege der Forschung* 419, complementing Ernst and Neuser on rhyme.

Klingenberg, H. *Runenschrift-Schriftdenken-Runeninschriften*. Heidelberg: Winter, 1973.

Lippert, J. *Beiträge zu Technik und Syntax althochdeutscher Übersetzungen*. Munich: Fink, 1974. Complex but interesting.

McKenzie, D. A. *Otfrid von Weissenburg: Narrator or Commentator*. Stanford: Stanford University Press, 1946. Useful survey of Otfrid's narrative method, in English.

Matzel, K. *Untersuchung zur Verfasserschaft, Sprache und Herkunft der althochdeutschen Isidor-Sippe*. Bonn: Röhrscheid, 1970.

Meissburger, G. *Grundlagen zum Verständnis der deutschen Mönchsdichtung im 11.*

und 12. Jahrhundert. Munich: Fink, 1970. Important, but see W. Schröder's comments in *ZfdA* 100 (1971):195–213.

Michel, P., and Schwarz, A. *Unz in obanentig.* Bonn: Bouvier, 1978. A close examination of exegetical writers and Otfrid at work.

Minis, C. *Handschrift, Form und Sprache des Muspilli.* Berlin: Erich Schmidt, 1966. Good, if not entirely convincing, reconstruction, with proper attention to the manuscript.

Mohr, W., and Haug, W. *Zweimal Muspilli.* Tübingen; Niemeyer, 1977. An exceptionally stimulating pair of brief essays.

Naumann, H. *Das Ludwigslied und die verwandten lateinischen Gedichte.* Halle: Klinz, 1932. Remains an important study, placing the German poem into a context.

Norman, F. *Three Essays on the Hildebrandslied.* Edited by A. T. Hatto. London: Institute of Germanic Studies, 1973. Stimulating, if not always acceptable, as interpretations.

Opitz, S. *Südgermanische Runeninschriften im älteren Futhark aus der Merowingerzeit.* Kirchzarten: Burg, 1977. Full study and collection/edition of the texts.

Ostberg, K. *The Old High German Isidor and its Relationship to the Extant Manuscripts (8.-12. Cent.) of Isidore's De Fide Catholica.* Göppingen: Kümmerle, 1979. Detailed survey.

Patzlaff, R. *Otfrid von Weissenburg und die mittelalterliche versus-Tradition.* Tübingen: Niemeyer, 1975. Interesting, if not completely conclusive, discussion of the origins of Otfrid's rhymes.

Pongs, H. *Das Hildebrandslied.* Marburg: Hütter, 1913. Still useful on manuscript.

Rupp, H. *Deutsche religiöse Dichtungen des 11. und 12. Jahrhunderts.* 2d ed. Berne and Munich: Francke, 1971. General study and chapters on *Ezzos Gesang* and others.

Schlosser, H. D. *Die literarischen Anfänge der deutschen Sprache.* Berlin: Erich Schmidt, 1977. Interesting approach.

Schulz, K. *Art und Herkunft des variierenden Stils in Otfrids Evangeliendichtung.* Munich: Fink, 1968. Good analysis of Otfrid's stylistic devices.

Schupp, V. *Studien zu Williram von Ebersberg.* Berne and Munich: Francke, 1978. Various aspects of Williram examined.

Schwab, U. *Arbeo laosa. Philologische Studien zum Hildebrandslied.* Berne: Francke, 1972. Excellent survey of research on points of linguistic interpretation.

———. *Die Sternrune im Wessobrunner Gebet.* Amsterdam: Rodopi, 1973. Basic study of the manuscript.

Sonderegger, S. *Althochdeutsch in St Gallen.* St Gallen: Ostschweiz, 1970. Good on the smaller survivals.

———. *Althochdeutsche Sprache und Literatur.* Berlin: de Gruyter, 1974. Handy introduction to grammar and to the texts.

Sperl, H. *Naturalismus und Idealismus in der althochdeutschen Literatur.* Published Ph.D. dissertation, Erlangen, 1927. Farfetched in some respects on the *Hildebrandslied,* but interesting on the *Ludwigslied* and the *Georgslied.*

Splett, J. *Abrogans-Studien.* Wiesbaden: Steiner, 1976. Very detailed study indeed of the individual entries.

————. *Samanunga-Studien.* Göppingen: Kümmerle, 1979.

Urmoneit, E. *Der Wortschatz des Ludwigsliedes im Umkreis der althochdeutschen Literatur.* Munich: Fink, 1973. Very detailed.

Vollmann-Profe, G. *Kommentar zu Otfrids Evangelienbuch. Teil I.* Bonn: Habelt, 1976. Useful on the Liutbert-letter.

3. Articles

Bacon, I. "Versuch einer Klassifizierung altdeutscher Zaubersprüche und Segen." *MLN* 67 (1952):224–32. Useful.

Baesecke, G. "Die altdeutschen Beichten." *PBB* 49 (1925):268–355. Monograph-length article surveying all the material.

————. "*Muspilli* II." *ZfdA* 82 (1948/50):199–239. Controversial, but important paper.

Berg, E. "Das *Ludwigslied* und die Schlacht bei Saucourt." *RVjb* 29 (1964):175–99. Extremely important paper, containing in addition a text of the poem by R. Schützeichel.

Bergmann, R. "Zu der althochdeutschen Inschrift aus Köln." *RVjb* 30 (1965):66–69. Brief but interesting on date and text.

Bischoff, B. "Paläographische Fragen deutscher Denkmäler der Karolingerzeit." *Frühmittelalterliche Studien* 5 (1971):101–34. Comments on the dating of most of the texts in their manuscript form.

Dittrich, M.-L. "*De Heinrico.*" *ZfdA* 84 (1952/3):274–308.

————. "Die literarische Form von Willirams *Expositio in Cantica Canticorum.*" *ZfdA* 84 (1952/3):179–97. Compare with the book by V. Schupp.

Gamber, K. "Das altbairische *Petruslied.*" In: *Festschrift F. Haberl.* Regensburg: Bosse, 1977, pp. 107–16. A survey.

Genzmer, F. "Germanische Zaubersprüche," *Germanisch-Romanische Monatsschrift* 32 (1950), 21–35. Useful for an overview.

Harvey, R. "The Provenance of the Old High German *Ludwigslied.*" *Medium Aevum* 14 (1945):1–20. A lucid study of the background.

Hatto, A. T. "On the Excellence of the *Hildebrandslied.*" *Modern Language Review* 68 (1973):820–38. A comparison with the other major versions of the father-son battle.

Homann, H. "Das *Ludwigslied*—Dichtung im Dienste der Politik?" In: *Studies in Honor of H. Jantz.* Munich: Delp, 1972, pp. 17–28. Interesting attempt to place the poem into a context.

Howard, J. A. "Über die Echtheit eines althochdeutschen Wiegenliedes."

Studia Neophilologica 48 (1976):21–35. See the comment in the following issue, 49 (1977):138.

Huisman, J. A. "Die Pariser Gespräche." *RVjb* 33 (1969):272–96. The best analysis of a difficult document.

Kienast, R. "Zur frühesten deutschen Kunstprosa." In: *Festschrift W. Stammler.* Berlin: Erich Schmidt, 1953, pp. 11–24. Good on Isidore-translation.

Kuhn, H. "Stoffgeschichte, Tragik und formaler Aufbau im *Hildebrandslied.*" In his *Text und Theorie.* Stuttgart: Metzler, 1969, pp. 113–25. Thought-provoking discussion.

McLintock, D. R. "The Politics of the *Hildebrandslied.*" *New German Studies* 2 (1974):61–81. An interesting reading of the work.

————. "*Himmel und Hölle.* Bemerkungen zum Wortschatz." In: *Studien zur frühmittelhochdeutschen Literatur.* Edited by L. P. Johnson et al. Berlin: Erich Schmidt, 1974, pp. 83–102.

Maurer, F. "*Hildebrandslied* und *Ludwigslied.*" *Der Deutschunterricht* 9, no. 2 (1957):5–15. Brief but extremely useful comparison.

Murdoch, B. "Saucourt and the *Ludwigslied.*" *Revue Belge de Philologie et d'Histoire* 55 (1977):841–67. The German poem and its narrator in an historical and theological context.

Rupp, H. "Der Neubeginn der deutschen religiösen Dichtung um die Mitte des 11. Jahrhunderts." *Wirkendes Wort* 8 (1957):268–76. Introducing early Middle High German literature.

Schröder, W. "Der Geist von Cluny und die Anfänge des frühmittelhochdeutschen Schrifttums." *PBB* 72 (1950):321–86. Important comments on the supposed religious motivation of German literature in the eleventh century.

Schröder, W. "Grenzen und Möglichkeiten einer althochdeutschen Literaturgeschichte." *Berichte . . . der sächsischen Akademie der Wissenschaften* (Leipzig), phil.-hist. K1. 105/ii (1959). Extremely important consideration of Old High German as a whole.

Schwarz, W. "The *Ludwigslied.* A Ninth-Century Poem." *Modern Language Review* 42 (1947):467–73. Brief but useful.

Sonderegger, S. "Frühe übersetzungsschichten im Althochdeutschen." In: *Festschrift W. Henzen.* Berne: Francke, 1965, pp. 101–14. Stimulating study of the earliest types of translation.

————. "Die Frage nach Notkers des Deutschen Ausgangspunkt." In: *Medievalia Litteraria. Festschrift H. de Boor.* Munich: Beck, 1971, pp. 119–33. Clarifies Notker's aims.

————. "Gesprochene Sprache im Althochdeutschen." in: *Ansätze zu einer pragmatischen Sprachgeschichte.* Edited by H. Sitte. Tübingen: Niemeyer, 1978, pp. 71–88, 132–34. Asks a number of interesting questions relating primarily to Notker.

Stavenhagen, L. "Das *Petruslied.*" *Wirkendes Wort* 17 (1967):21–28. A discussion of the problems of the text, manuscript transmission and music.

Wehrli, M. "Gattungsgeschichtliche Betrachtungen zum *Ludwigslied.*" In his *Formen mittelalterlichen Erzählung.* Freiburg i. Br.: Atlantis, 1969, pp. 73–86. A clear-headed look at some of the ways in which different aspects have been overemphasized in the interpretation of the poem.

Willems, F. "Psalm 138 and althochdeutscher Stil." *Deutsche Vierteljahresschrift* 29 (1955):429–46. Clear study of the work.

Index